D1520772

HEAVEN'S PASSPORT
For a Fuller Life on Earth

by
Carnegie Samuel Calian

Other Books by C.S. Calian

Today's Pastor in Tomorrow's World

The Significance of Eschatology in the Thoughts of Nicholas Berdyaev

Berdyaev's Philosophy of Hope

Icon and Pulpit: The Protestant-Orthodox Encounter

Grace, Guts and Goods: How to Stay Christian in an Affluent Society

The Gospel according to *The Wall Street Journal*

For All Your Seasons: Biblical Directions through Life's Passages

Where's the Passion for Excellence in the Church?

Theology Without Boundaries: Encounters of Eastern

Orthodoxy and Western Tradition

Survival or Revival: Ten Keys to Church Vitality

The Ideal Seminary: Pursuing Excellence in
Theological Education
The Spirit-Driven Leader: Seven Keys to Succeeding
Under Pressure

Heaven's Passport
ISBN: 9798674214755

Table of Contents

To Doris on our sixty-first wedding anniversary, with our heartfelt thanks to a gracious God for family, friends and strangers too, who have loved us in so many ways with kindness & hospitality, adding meaning to our lives.

Concept: Why a Biblical Passport?

Passports have two basic aspects. At a legal level, they serve as a credential that certifies the right of the bearer to enter, at least temporarily, another sovereign country. They are a kind of license to be somewhere else. But at another, more personal level, they authenticate who we are, identifying us as a particular and unique member of the human race. At a time when political authorities across the globe, fanned by the flames of nationalism and so-called "strategic interests", are erecting new barriers to the free movement of people, ideas and especially shared hopes for peace, justice, and equality, all aspects of passports have taken on growing importance.

It is the authenticating role of these dossiers that has intrigued me the most. We live in the twenty-first century world beset by wars, famine, unprecedented social and political upheavals, as well as cataclysmic climate change and pandemics. In today's globalized, technological society, we are wired together, but also more spiritually disconnected than at any time in human history. Need it be this way forever? Several years ago, I began to pose the question of whether all of us could benefit from developing passports that further personalize who we are and encompass the spirited dimension of our identity. Amidst the perplexities and challenges of contemporary life, could each of us—as Christians, Jews, Muslims, Hindus, Buddhists, and practitioners of other faiths—benefit from carrying along with our bound and stamped booklet another less tangible, but no less proof of our core beliefs?

That is how my own biblical passport took shape. And it gained specificity and weight as I reflected on the notion that each of us, no matter what our nationality or background, is created in God's image, the *imago Dei,* with all that implies about our lives to be spiritually empowered to leave the world a better, more just, and humane place honoring God's creation.

In the pages of **HEAVEN'S PASSPORT *for a fuller life on earth,*** I have tried to model the central elements for a faith-centered way of engaging with friends, neighbors, strangers, and even adversaries. My book draws extensively on the Bible and my understanding of sacred texts shaped by a long career as minister, educator, seminary and university professor in theology, ethics and leadership. The book is intended not only for believers but for seekers who may have lost—or never had—an abiding religious faith. My hope is that readers will use this book not only as a resource for strengthening their own inner sense of living under God's grace, but also as *one's biblical passport* for getting acquainted on trips.

"Be the change you want to see."
-Mahatma Gandhi

"Finish what you started in me, God. Your love is eternal—don't quit on me now."
-Psalm 138:8, The *Message: The Bible in Contemporary Language,* Eugene H. Peterson, NavPress

"Do not put your trust in princes, in mortals, in whom there is no help. When their breath departs, they return to the earth; on that very day their plans perish."
-Psalm.146:3-4, *The New Oxford Annotated Bible*

Preface: How I Began My Biblical Passport

The idea of possessing a biblical passport came to me as I was examining my updated U.S. Passport at home for a forthcoming trip when invited to serve as a volunteer chaplain on the Holland America Line. Sitting before me was my bookshelf with different biblical translations I have found useful in my classes with clergy, laity, and the ship's ecumenical crew of diverse employees. It was then that I envisioned having my own biblical passport that would accompany my U.S. passport on our ports-of-call circumnavigating the world. My biblical passport would be brief, enabling me to commit basic points to memory for easy use as I shared my values in relation to my experiences in life. As the world's global community expands, it will take time to feel relaxed, to gain one another's trust. The following is my seven-point model for a *biblical passport* for my use at home and in travels abroad.

1. Start Your Day Right (Psalms 139:23-24)

My own biblical passport begins with a scriptural prayer from the Psalms: *"Search me, O God, and know my heart; test me and know my thoughts. See if there is any wicked way in me and lead me in the way everlasting."* This is my morning prayer (*New Revised Standard Version*) My quiet time also includes other Bible readings, reflections and giving thanks to God for another day of grace, whatever the weather might be. This is followed by a two-mile morning walk at the nearby high school's football field with two retired coaches—Bob and Harry and my wife Doris who joins us occasionally when she is not swimming. This is a time for fellowship and the exchanging of ideas before jogging. We discuss many news events (the Penn State gym coach's inappropriate conduct, tragic shootings in Colorado, Connecticut, Texas, Florida, etc., presidential and global politics, and recent interviews conducted by newscasters on television.) We also mention recent Hollywood films and community programs. Of course, we question one another often, reflecting our biases and respective outlooks on life, faith and death. We might even admit wryly that we have learned something; although no one seems to come around entirely to my way of thinking. That's fine with me, since we all can be wrong at times.

2. Treat Individuals as Sacred (Galatians 5:6). The risk of getting acquainted with complete strangers as fellow humans is an essential first step in developing partnerships, discovering what values we can share even when speaking from different cultural backgrounds. We learn to lift up one another's hopes through a caring word and perhaps a cup of tea or coffee to begin to understand that we are fellow human beings. We need to transcend today's barriers, placed there, we are told, for our protection, but often curtailing our learning in this age of transparency. To see matters clearly is to realize that individuals are much more than a means to another's purpose. But will this awareness move us toward a set of common convictions when we discuss and design the contents of our individual passports, uncovering a range of values shared in building a wiser global community in our lifetime? Today's global population deserves far more respect than to be manipulated away from the spiritual core of humanity. We are created in God's image (*the imago Dei* from Genesis 1: 26-27 to 2:4) which claims our collective humanity under our Creator-God. Unfortunately, too many humans around the world are feeling less human today. As human beings, who have the creative potential to work together; we can do better. We are expected to mature and enjoy life as well as our families and friends, enlarging our circle of fellowship to include strangers and also competitors and enemies at times. Otherwise, what hope have we for lasting peace, prosperity or justice as a global community? It would be a relevant study for biblical readers to return to Paul's Letter in Galatians 5: 22-26, often referred to as the *"Magna Carta of Christian liberty",* reminding people of faith that, *"Neither circumcised nor uncircumcised counts for anything; the only thing that counts is faith working through love."* (New Revised Standard Version)

3. **Be Generous (Acts 4:32 – 5:11).** In the Acts of the Apostles, we learn that the early community of believers was strengthened and grew through its spirit of generosity. Property and other possessions were given to the community to sell, and the general funds were later distributed according to each member's need. Based on the community's rules, Ananias and Sapphira agreed to unite with the early church, pledging their property as was the custom, to assist the congregation in its welfare ministry that benefited the larger community's life and needs. Later when their joint property was actually sold, they decided to hold back a major portion of the proceeds from the sale without gaining permission from the apostles and the congregation. Thus, they cheated on the rules of the community which had welcomed them. They chose to hedge their bets, experiencing the benefits of church membership without paying the full cost of commitment. Subsequently, their

cheating became known; they paid for their lying with their lives. *(King James Version)*

4. **Practice Moderation (Galatians 5:22-23).** Moderation is more difficult to maintain than we may think. We can become addicted to many forms of temptations that hit us like an unexpected storm. We are left totally unprepared in a state of chaos. It can be said that we are as wise and ethical as the last time we were tempted. None of us is truly immune from these situations. Obsession in its many forms seems to trample our best intentions. But when we practice moderation, as the Bible encourages, we find ourselves happily engaged in tasting the fruits of the Spirit which consist of "love, joy, peace, patience, generosity, faithfulness, gentleness, and self-control. There is no law against such things." The discipline of moderation becomes a significant ethical key releasing joy in our lives, enabling us to rejoice in healthy relationships far beyond our expectations. *(New Revised Standard Version)*

5. **Disclose Mistakes (Mark 4:22-23).** Confession and restitution are necessary to restore ethical character throughout the global community. The news today is full of apologies, blame and cheating, but such practices leave us dissatisfied and issues largely unresolved. Furthermore, such behavior thwarts healthy relationships, true

healing, and authentic forgiveness. Unresolved feuds can last for generations among families, societies and nations. Religious disputes aren't any better. In many cases, our errors are buried, but not forgotten. Saints are often sinners revised and edited for the benefit of any organization's morale. Mark's Gospel (4:22-23) has it right when Jesus warns his disciples saying, "For there is nothing hidden but it must be disclosed; nothing kept secret except to be brought to light. If anyone has ears to hear, let him listen to this." *(The Jerusalem Bible).*

6. **Speak Briefly, and Act Wisely (I Kings 3:27-28).** False information destroys credibility and clouds our judgment. This is dangerous. Lies are endemic to our lives; even etiquette fosters deceit in our relationships. Speaking the truth in practice is not exactly a science; it is an artful as well as an ethical matter in dealing with all persons involved in our lives and in human affairs. To act wisely in delicate matters affecting the lives of others requires that leaders stay well-informed, not driven by rumor or anger, but rather by the facts. Having all the evidence before making judgments may be impossible. But we are obligated to maximize our knowledge as a prerequisite for coming to a just appraisal. This is never easy in the heat of emotions from all sides of the issue. Take the case of King Solomon soon after he assumed the throne following the long

reign of King David. Everyone in the assembly hall watched as two prostitutes were brought before Solomon, each woman claimed motherhood of the child presented to the king. Each had given birth, but one child had died, and the babies were switched – or were they? Which woman is now telling the truth –which is lying? The crowd becomes silent as each woman makes her case before the king. The young King Solomon turned to his guard ordering the baby to be cut in two, one-half to be given to each woman. The true mother cried out to the king to save the child, yielding the baby to the other woman. She loved the child too much to see the baby killed. Then Solomon said, "Give the living baby to this woman; do not kill it. She is its mother." And the people of Israel saw that their king had divine wisdom and the ability to administer justice. *(The New English Bible)*

7. **Don't Quit on God, Others & Yourself (Psalm 138).** This admonition is directed to those of us who worry too much about ourselves. When the waters of life are stormy, we have that scary feeling that perhaps God is absent. Like a ship unexpectedly encountering a hurricane at sea, as happened to us and more than a thousand passengers and crew at Cape Horn en route to Antarctica. At the time, Doris and I were studying in the ship's library. I was preparing the next day's worship service as the Protestant

chaplain onboard, when two 80-foot waves in quick succession splashed the window and sent us, along with chairs, tables, books, etc. across the room. It was a very frightening experience. The ship was like a cork surrounded by high waves as the dedicated captain and crew made every effort to head back to port some distance away. Dishes in the dining room and much of the furniture were broken. Amidst the anxiety and fear, many found themselves praying. The next day, when calm set in, we experienced an overflowing worship service in the ship's theater to everyone's joy. The "Easter crowd" was back in church. For a moment during the storm, many felt that God had quit on us.

We may presently have neighbors and family members who feel like that, filled with anxieties and worries from economic fears, job concerns, poverty and health needs, in addition to the displacement of refugees around the world. More recently we have been globally hit by the COVID-19 pandemic, which has made us aware again that fellow sufferers live in a world without borders, having a common kinship related to the *imago Dei beckoning us to be involved*, fulfilling our stewardship to God.

Major questions of life face all of us: How caring will we be to others when tested? What will be our order of priorities? Who will we serve first and why, when there is hardly any time or sufficient funds to stock and share what's needed whether at home or abroad?

My model of a biblical passport closes with Psalm 138 as an abiding note of comfort in the midst of life's unanswered questions. Namely, to start and end everyday of our lives in a spirit of gratitude, reminding ourselves that we live by God's grace hopefully surrounded by loving relationships known and even unknown to us at times. It is these spiritual realities that enable us to face life's journeys empowered not to quit on God, others, or ourselves when tempted to do so. This is why the Psalmist prays so powerfully, *"When I walk into the thick of trouble, keep me alive in the angry turmoil. With one hand, strike my foes; with your other hand, save me. Finish what you started in me, God. Your love is eternal, don't quit on me now." (Psalm 138: 7-8 from Eugene Peterson's The Message: The Bible in Contemporary Language.*

Part I: Start Your Day Right

Chapter 1. Worship God Truthfully

God spoke, "You shall have no other gods before me." (Exodus 20:3). Worship services are those special occasions for us to renew and review truthfully our commitment to our biblical God who is jealous of all rivals competing for our devotion. We humans are inescapable worshippers; as a consequence, there exists the perpetual temptation of turning our idols into gods unworthy of our lasting embrace. We tend to be either too judgmental or too tolerant at times. Nevertheless, we defend our freedom of curiosity as we sample one "god" after another. When we are honest with ourselves, most seem to belong to today's generation of seekers in some ways, unwilling to admit it publicly perhaps among fellow believers. Many religious seekers tend to be short-term rather than long-term believers. This may explain the growing tide of rootless spirituality in current society. This may also indicate why we are no longer loyal to any single tradition. Various surveys report that over 90% of the population believe in "God," yet church attendance among mainline Protestant traditions (but also among Catholics and Evangelicals), continues to decline. No doubt there will be changes ahead from lessons learned during the pandemic. Furthermore, the "God" that 90% believe in may be a far contrast to the true biblical God. To examine with discernment which "God" deserves our trust is a challenging task facing houses of worship and theological schools of all traditions in the coming decades of this century.

Churches and seminaries dedicated to worshipping and interpreting the biblical God are committed to distinguishing their God from the many "false gods" in the market- place. Even so, many believers regard the task of naming the "right God" to be solely an autonomous subjective pursuit of the individual without the aid of ecclesiastical institutions (as many "Nones" do today). As a result, we have actually increased public interest in spirituality with television angels and spiritual films from Hollywood describing "god" to us, a description that may or not correspond with the biblical God. It is these popular images of the supernatural that further confuse us as we gather to praise the biblical God of Abraham, Sarah, Mary, Joseph and Jesus, recognized by students of the Bible and the public in general.

Worship services ought to be designed to usher us immediately into the presence of the biblical God who awaits our praise and seeks to address the many anxieties and ambiguities of life. Is this happening in today's worship experience? Is worship providing the opportunity for a divine encounter? Perhaps our praise and study of God is too closely associated with the music and style of our "cultural wars" of today, leading us away from an authentic worship experience. Is the use of the latest media technology in worship an enhancement or a barrier in our desire to actualize God's presence in worship? Jim Taylor, writing in *Perspectives*, humorously asks the question, "Is technology a blessing or a curse?" He illustrates by saying: "I started wondering what might happen if God copied modern technology and installed voice-mail. I imagined something like this:

"Hello," says an angelic voice. "Thank you for calling heaven. We value your prayer and will make every effort to take care of your concerns promptly and efficiently. Please stay on the line; we can deal with your prayers more quickly then, rather than to hang up and try again. To help us direct your call to the party to whom you wish to speak, please route your call as follows: If you wish to speak to one of the martyrs, press 1; to one of the saints, press 2; to one of the angels, press 3; to the Virgin Mary, press 4; to Jesus, press 5; to the Holy Spirit press 6; and if you wish to speak directly to God, press 7.

I pressed 7. I wanted to go right to the top. Beep and beep again. There was a long pause. The telephone line played a recording of Bruce Springsteen singing a Bach cantata accompanied by a choir comprising 2,000 voice clones of Linda Ronstadt. Then a voice came on that was neither male nor female, neither loud nor soft. In

29

fact, I couldn't even give it a quality – it seemed to vibrate through the very molecules of nature and permeate my cells and my thoughts. I knew it must, at last be God. 'Thank you for calling,' the voice said. 'Your call is very important to me. I'm sorry, but I'm either away from my heavenly throne or tied up with another prayer request. If you wish to speak to my secretary, press zero. Otherwise, please leave a detailed message at the sound of the harp, and I'll get back to you as soon I can.'"

While many explanations have been given for the decline in church membership and attendance, my suspicion is that the church has become increasingly less relevant to its own members. The dropouts from church may also be due to boredom and intolerance of mediocre worship services which often can't be distinguished from weekly service club meetings promoting public and business interests or community and professional concerns. For others, church has become simply a series of political causes where like-minded individuals seek to advance their favorite cause. Large church assemblies often display numerous advocacy booths. Some lose interest in the church when their personal cause no longer receives attention.

Many still continue to attend church regularly. They are attracted to the inspiring quality of musical performances and preaching experienced. Professionalism in these high-performance churches has turned congregations into audiences seeking entertainment. Many know that minimal commitment is demanded of the audience, which boils down to financial support. The other significant factor that draws many persons to church is the fellowship they enjoy even if it is sometimes spoiled when questionable strangers wish to join. Of course, there are exceptions to these generalizations, thank God! Hopefully, the religious groups we are associated with are among those joyful congregations which present a visionary spirit to energize everyone. Others may envision virtual gatherings in our post-pandemic era.

The God of Grace and Mystery

Worshipping God and serving others may not be enough to satisfy a meaningful journey of faith. In honesty, we may still hunger and yearn for a deeper relation to God. Perhaps we seek some kind of mystical ecstasy or union with God where our personal tragedies are addressed, where unanswered questions are faced-- "Why me, Lord?" However, I'm afraid most of us will continue to encounter puzzling ambiguities and victimization from racism, poverty, sexual orientation, aging, broken homes and many other unfortunate and unexplained tragedies. We will still be immersed in "cultural wars". Our old enemies will be replaced by newer ones, and our moments of peace will be interrupted by conflict and loneliness. In any case, we are urged to move forward by the grace of God.

We long for greater harmony and wholeness in our lives; but quite frankly, no church or theological education can guarantee the certainty that we long for and desire daily. With increasing disappointment, a growing number in our society have opted for an uncommitted lifestyle, an open highway without signs and leading to dead ends. Since everything is seemingly subject to change, they refuse to engage in any long-term spiritual commitments. If only God would give quick, bite-size responses that provide wisdom to unanswered questions. Is God deaf to our sound-bite oriented society? Our attention span isn't long; we yearn to close the gap between asking questions and finding answers. It is sad but true that many in our communities perceive churches and seminaries to be sources of confusion rather than clarity. Society looks for two-minute spiritual recipes (a panacea) with a divine confirmation through email or voicemail. Yet to survive as human beings, a coherent sense of meaning is needed at the very core of our lives. Responsible religious education in our houses of worship as well as seminaries, colleges and university classrooms offer direction to soothe discontented spirits, leading to pathways of hope.

St. Augustine maintained that a restlessness within us struggles to make peace with God. But until we have reached our mountain top experience with God, we will continue to be tossed to and fro on a stormy sea with only our questioning faith, weak though it may be at times, as our lifeline between us and God. We continue to struggle with doubts, encouraged and thankful from time to time for those grace-filled moments of God's presence in our lives. Religious writer Frederick Buechner confessed some time ago at a General Assembly of Presbyterians that he was no longer a regular churchgoer. "I hate to say this," said Buechner, "but for many years now I've taken to going to church less and less, because I find so little there of what I hunger for...it's a sense of the presence of God that I hunger for. It's grace that I hunger for." Can you identify with Buechner?

To me, this deeper experience of God's grace in worship can still be had if we suspend judgment on the confused feelings within us. We can create our own moments of tranquility while seated or kneeling prayerfully, seeking divine wisdom to gradually quiet us with spiritual comfort. This quietness can stir our souls to enjoy peace and communion with God knowing that we are no longer alone. Unfortunately, in posturing with one another and disappointment with fellow believers, our energy to pursue a deeper relationship with God has declined. The grace-filled moments elude us. Fortunately, there are still times when we realize that God has not let go--ushering us into fleeting seconds of divine ecstasy as our spirits are lifted to see a rainbow of hope after the storm.

We need to know that we can still add moments of hope as we submit ourselves to do God's Will by building forgiving relationships with one another where authentic and caring trust prevails. The recovery of authentic relationships, divine and human, is the essence of God's agenda for the People of God. *God is in the business of reconciliation.*

Frankly, I wonder if God is tired of hearing our prayers for survival. Instead, let's pray for a fresh vision of a fuller life that frees us from our addictions and self-imprisoned barriers. Peter and Cornelius (Acts 10) were each praying in their separate places revealing their cultural differences, but both received a similar vision of the *imago Dei* from God's Spirit that dynamically transformed their outlooks, enabling them to cross the psychic boundaries that divide and separate so many believers and seekers today. Their shared vision at that moment was indeed a grace-filled moment for Peter and Cornelius. We need more encounters like this in our post-pandemic interconnected world in need.

We need to realize that preaching, singing, praying and blaming will not unveil the divine mystery to us. Neither will a traditional, non-traditional, nor even a blended service can satisfy us fully. Nor will a study of theology mixed with traditional dogmas from several respective traditions reveal the divine essence to us. For that matter, any study of theology per se without humility may lead to ignorance and abstract propositions that are no more than mere speculations. Finite categories of human understanding cannot capture God's true being. *We are engaged in a faith journey.* Our convictions are humbly woven with

34

doubts. The few answers we have may not correspond neatly to every tragedy we face, nor will our "answer" stand up to empirical and rational measurements in our present finite status.

In the meantime, one can still hold on to the simplicity and mystery of faith. This is because we are at peace with our shared trust in God's grace and guidance of our lives. Our finite trust in God is much like a baby's trust in loving and carrying parents. It is a far more satisfying experience than our attempts to explain everything rationally. Faith is an empowering experience that is fulfilling, but also leaves us with more questions than answers in our common quest for understanding our sacred texts and the unfolding journey of faith in the forgiving love of our Creator-God for the sake of humankind in a created world that continues to expand before us.

We also believe that God exists before the beginning of creation. This affirmation is expressed among believers in countless ways from their respective faiths. For Christians, the Divine Presence is incarnate (made flesh) in Jesus the Christ whose brief earthly ministry as God's son emphasized God's forgiving love to humankind and who continues to reign for our sakes as the resurrected Christ of faith and hope fulfilling the wishes of our Creator-God, that we too would walk in the spirit of the imago *Dei* as Jesus did, practicing forgiving love with one other, advancing God's kingdom, not ours.

Scripture to consider:
Psalm 23, 139:23-24; 90:1-17; 100:1-5, 118
Proverbs: Chapters 8, 9. & 10
Matthew 6:9-15; 7:1-28; 15:1-39; 16: 21-28
Luke 10:29-37
Romans 5: 1-21

Books, articles and films for classroom and neighborhood discussions:
Jurgen Moltmann, *The Trinity and The Kingdom: The Doctrine of God,* Harper & Row, New York and also *God In Creation: A New Theology of Creation And the Spirit of God*, Harper & Row

Hans Kung, *Tracing the Way: Spiritual Dimensions of the World Religions,* Continuum, London

Jack Miles, *GOD; A Biography; and Christ: A Crisis in the Life of God,* Alfred A. Knopf, New York. More recently, Miles completed his trilogy with, *GOD in The QUR'AN,* also published by Knopf.

Gabriel Said Reynolds, *The Qur'an & Bible: Text and Commentary*, Yale University Press

Robert Alter, *The Hebrew Bible: A Translation with Commentary* was published recently in three volumes in English by W.W. Norton

Reza Aslan, *God: A Human History,* Random House, New York

Robert Louis Wilken, ***LIBERTY in the Things of GOD: The Christian, Origins of Religious Freedom,*** Yale University Press. Professor Wilken reminds us of Lactantius, a fourth-century Christian writer's early observation*: "There is no room for force and violence because religion cannot be compelled. Let words be used rather than blows, that the decision may be free."*

God In America: How Religious Liberty Shaped America*,* DVD on PBS. This film is part of the documentary series from the award-winning producers of *American Experience* and *Frontline* with faculty members from the American Academy of Religion.

I AM is a story told by Hollywood director, Tom Shadyac. The film asks two basic questions: "What's wrong with our world? What can we do about it?

The Two Popes: a film designed as a historic encounter between Pope Benedict XVI and his likely successor at the time, Argentine Cardinal Jorge Bergoglio (today's Pope Francis) who was invited to meet privately for a series of dialogues on their respective outlooks on life with their contrasting cultural backgrounds.

Chapter 2. How Well Do We Know Ourselves?

Have you ever attended a seminary class? I recommend that you try it sometime and discover what is involved in developing pastoral, ethical and spiritual leadership in our accredited graduate institutions. In fact, I wish you had been present when the following discussion took place some years ago in my class at Seminary.

I asked the students that morning to put their materials and computers to one side, and to respond to the following question: What realistic assumption regarding human nature will you bring to your future church members? To put it simply, are you going to see people as basically good or as basically bad? In which direction will you place your emphasis? Our game-plan for the class today is to examine that question.

To begin the discussion, I asked the twenty-five students present to raise hands to indicate their position before the debate: "Are people basically good or basically bad?" I should admit to readers at the start, that theological issues (like political issues) are never really solved by a vote, but for the sake of having the total class involved in the morning's experiment, I repeated with added emphasis that we would be side-tracking for the moment important issues of fairness and injustice often asked in this process, as we sought to understand our human nature collectively.

Before I mention how the students voted, it would be interesting to test ourselves on this question. How many of us would be willing to declare publicly our position on human nature? I suspect some in my class had such feelings that morning. It was my hope that most would seize the moment as an opportunity to learn about themselves and the social context of their future ministry wherever that might lead. In short, how "authentic" do we dare to be? Such questions could also be raised as we prepare our individual biblical passports wherever we wish to travel.

Seventeen students in my class that morning voted that human nature is basically good; eight voted the opposite. Then our class discussion really took-off for what was an intense debate for the duration of our class session. As class time was ending, we all knew that the discussion was far from over. Following class, I had a luncheon engagement downtown with an active businessman. The heat from the classroom discussion was still with me when I arrived. I shared the dynamics of the past few hours with my friend. He patiently listened, then finally said, "Stop! Listen to my experience, before we need to leave." I anticipated a mini-sermon: "I want to predict to you," said my luncheon friend, "which of your students will become successful pastors.

He went on to say, "I didn't become successful by being unrealistic. I learned from my hard knocks with customers and avoided making the same mistake twice. Those seminarians that voted that human nature is basically bad, I predict are on the path to becoming successful pastors. Do you know why? These seminarians indicate to me by their vote that they understand the real world. Life is tough, and the temptation to cut corners is always there. It is part of our DNA, our human nature. It may also be why citizens in any society are willing to justify their risks, even having to steal or lie under pressure, defending their self-interest as well as their pride. In fact, there is truth in those old clichés that refer to society as a 'rat race' and a 'dog-eat-dog' environment. Those students that declare there is a propensity for being bad have a realistic outlook on human nature, even more so than they probably realize."

What my business friend had in mind was not simply main street, but the bigger picture of life, that has disappointed and displaced countless lives, increased prison population and Salvation Army relief, harmed our children and caused loss of human respect, destroying relationships and increasing distrust.

I have also noticed recently, that if anyone is still looking for help beyond the usual 48 hours of emergency aid, we begin to look upon that person as a possible leech. We tend to be suspicious of others, and often place limits on our own charity and goodwill.

Rabbi Harold Kushner's popular book *When Bad Things Happen to Good People* has captured the attention of believers from many faith traditions. Perhaps Rabbi Kushner has neglected, however, the other side of life's questions that confront us with equal force, *Why Do Good People Do Bad Things?* Our response to this question also needs to be addressed!

It is not my intention to denigrate ourselves, but to be realistic. There is some measure of caring in almost everyone. Otherwise what hope would we have in becoming goodwill ambassadors in today's emerging global society? *We are all created in God's image*, to live as soulmates to one another embedded as we are in the divine image of our Creator according to our sacred texts. Our distrust of one another reveals that this essential image has been tarnished. There are degrees of brokenness that prevail in many relationships at home and abroad. In scriptural readings, the Apostle Paul has clearly described the human situation as a constant struggle between one's will to do good countered by our inability to carry out those good intentions. *"I will attempt to do something worthwhile,"* says Paul, *"but find myself doing the opposite."* In short, we are contradictory creatures. The flaw in us is what biblical language calls *sin.* (Romans 7: 15-20)

No one can escape sin; we are all tainted. However, I am not interested solely in debating our tainted nature but wish to indicate our propensity to be contradictory. Sometimes the badness in us comes out as pride, stubbornness, arrogance, which we regret later. At other times it reveals itself in rather subversive actions as we create rationalizations for our behavior. Unless we are honest with ourselves, God's power to connect with our lives and fulfill us is frustrated. Among the Reformation leaders was theologian John Calvin who resided in Geneva, Switzerland. He stated clearly, *"Without knowledge of self, there is no knowledge of God."* Once we admit this, the passage to divine empowerment becomes a possibility wherever we live and work.

Churchgoers often repeat in their worship liturgy the "Confession of Our Sins." This declaration and pardon remind us that we have fallen short of the standards set by our Founder. So often this part of the liturgy becomes *pro forma* and is uttered without thought or authenticity. We have become too accustomed to the word *"sinner".* For example, I could have asked the seminarians in my class that morning, whether they truly regarded themselves as sinners? The voting pattern might have changed. We have become too comfortable and accustomed to hearing "sin language" as "church language" and respond automatically without any deeper reflection.

Many of us share a realistic sense that we are not perfect. Yet when we ask ourselves if we are "basically good" or "basically bad," we tend to see ourselves as "a good person" who may not be perfect, but we certainly aren't that *bad*. Yet the *Good News* among us is that God has nevertheless saved us in the midst of our tendency to emphasize our wills (and wishes) rather than *God's Will*. But have we acknowledged this reality within ourselves? This is the evangelistic message that the Rev. Billy Graham popularized globally to millions in his lifetime of ministry. How honest are we today about *our human nature* actually displayed in today's marketplace? Are we really doing anything to correct matters heard and read in the news?

Perhaps we are in a state of denial and offer excuses for our behavior and shortcomings. Too many are living mixed-up lives, compounded by political confusion and changing signals between right and wrong in our present interactions and expectations with one another. Are we no longer accountable under our Creator-God? Are we passing on fake news to one another as our right under free speech? Have we neglected our spiritual GPS? Are we in need of regaining direction in the midst of the fake signs misguiding our souls in matters of truth, justice, and peacemaking? Will our biblical passports assist us in correcting matters? How bold will goodwill ambassadors be in situations to restore order across borders? *How well do we know ourselves medically, economically, sexually and spiritually today?*

I had been invited to speak at a large conference of religious leaders in the Midwest, when a participant stood up and waved his program of activities for the day in our faces saying, "Every Sunday when I go to church," he said, "the usher offers me a church bulletin. As I sit down to read it, the printed confession of our sins flashes before me, and no matter how beautifully written it may be each week, the bottom line tells me I am a lousy guy. I don't buy that, and I never will!"

"Sure," he continued, "I blow my top at times, but who doesn't? Sure, I know I am not the perfect father at home, but who is? What I do know," he said, "is that I am trying; and I want to get some credit for that!" And then he sat down.

If we accept that speaker's logic, we will soon be asking ourselves why do we need church at all? Perhaps that is how a growing number are feeling and thinking today. Perhaps there's no need for forgiveness or a Savior. We can buy our own coffee and do our trust-building exercises elsewhere, where at least some individuals seem more authentic rather than those encountered in religious houses of worship where fellowship with the "right people" is so selective. What feelings will we have in our post-pandemic period ahead?

How much fiction can we afford in life? Admittedly, we all need some fiction in our daily living; as we sip our first cup of coffee in the morning almost naked or without any make-up. Don't most of us as we mature need some fictional aids to help us face life –from shaving in the morning to cosmetics, to scented deodorant, to the clothes we wear, and to the final look at the magic mirror as we leave the house or apartment.

Some fiction we may all need; how *much* is another question. When does too much fiction become unhealthy for our well-being, separating us from the *real* world? How much fiction are we willing to include in our biblical passports? None of us will feel protected behind a biblical passport that is no more than a bubble-wrap cushioning our true character. At any time, one's protective face-cover of a biblical passport could be lifted or invaded unexpectedly by the harshness and ugliness of our inhumanity toward one another. In such moments of crisis, will we find the courage to be counted as goodwill ambassadors with our biblical passport in hand for guidance? Will we choose to be naïve and hope our testing will pass quickly, enabling us to return to our superficial etiquette that has been a part of our life journey so far.

Every believer's faith can be both realistic and hopeful. The crosses we wear around our necks invite us to face life and view it with joy as well as pain. Most will not live up to our potential, created as we are in the image of God *(the imago Dei)*, but we can all make a start by being honest with ourselves as we learn some basic lessons in humility, enabling God's Spirit to instill caring love of others as we strengthen our spiritual backbone.

For me, my quiet time with God begins most mornings, as I arise from bed and do reading and prayer, rekindling the grace of divine empowerment within me and enabling me to admit my weaknesses, misjudgments, and contradictions. I find this disciplined routine an opportunity to be honest before God and those I plan to meet during the day along with the unexpected that occurs. I am energized by God's Spirit to do and to say what is right as I pray in silence for wisdom and humility, and for a fulfilling day. Otherwise, I would probably fall flat on my face. That can easily happen whenever I fail to listen sufficiently or get carried away with my own stories, forgetting to listen to family, friends and critics with discernment and thoughtfulness.

In the ongoing task of knowing ourselves more fully, we must ask ourselves two ongoing questions: *First, is it our wish to continue to be naïve as we face the real world? Second, are we willing to learn something new in an effort to expand our encounters, readings, and capacity to listen and learn wisely?* The answers to these primary questions will remain throughout our lifetime. As we agonize to be honest, we will discover as did the Apostle Paul, the unending depth of God's love which enriches us on our journeys, enlarging our perspective to envision *God's Will, not ours,* as primary in our focus to advance the divine purpose for our lives. We will also feel the continued need to update our biblical passports as we become wiser goodwill ambassadors engaged in furthering the divine will of our Creator's expanding universe.

Scripture to consider:
Psalm 37
Proverbs 6: 16-19 (what the Lord hates)
Ecclesiastes 1, 2, & 3
Matthew 7
Romans 7: 14-8:2

Books, articles and films for classroom and neighborhood discussions:
Reinhold Niebuhr, *Moral Man and Immoral Society*, Scribner's Sons, New York

Joshua Wolf Shenk, Lincoln's *Melancholy: How Depression Challenged a President and Fueled His Greatness*, Houghton Mifflin Company, Boston

Tsedal Neeley, *The Language of Global Success*, Princeton, New Jersey. This book is about Hiroshi Mikitani, CEO of a large Japanese company, Rakuten, which trans- formed the language of the organization from Japanese to English in a two-year time period because Mikitani understood his business and co-workers in need of change.

David A. Light, A *Conversation with the Reverend Peter J. Gomes, Harvard* pastor for the University community. The conversation with Dr. Gomes asks the question, "Is Success A Sin"? Peter W. Marty, publisher of *The Christian Century* writes on a related theme, *"Shaping the Conscience"* (8/ 30/17) raising the question every reformer of society like Martin Luther King carried, *"Is it right?"* Eilene Zimmerman, *"Gossip Is Information By Another Name"*, *NYTimes*, *11/2/08* Editorial Opinion, *"The Poor, the Near Poor and You"*, *NYTimes*, 11/24/11

Two recent films and a play for discussion: *Darkest Hour is* a film on Winston Churchill and the beginning of World War II, and the film *The Post* is on Katherine Graham, the publisher of *The Washington* Post and her struggle with President Richard Nixon concerning the freedom of the press during the Vietnam War. Both films struggle with issues of national self-understanding, freedom & democracies. The performance of a timely mystery play "Six Corners" by Keith Huff centers on the Chicago Police Department, raising an underlying public question among citizens, *"Are cops a force for good"?*

Beverly Gage, *Core Values, The New York Times Magazine,* February 10, 2019. Gage discusses the question, "Has American politics—polarized, dysfunctional and averse to compromise—lost its *'center'?*

Chapter 3. Life's Purpose: Upholding the *imago Dei* in Us

Many of us are familiar with the comic strip *Peanuts* created by Charles Schulz. Not long ago, a classic reprint of *Peanuts* appeared in our Sunday papers. You may have seen it. Snoopy is sitting on a tree stump with his typewriter, writing the story of his life as seen through the eyes of his make-believe hero. This is what Snoopy writes:

"And so, our hero's life ended as it had begun…a disaster 'I never get any breaks' he had always complained. He had wanted to be rich. He died poor. He wanted friends. He died friendless. He wanted to be loved. He died unloved. He wanted laughter. He found only tears. He wanted applause. He received boos. He wanted fame. He found only obscurity. He wanted answers. He found only questions." And then Snoopy, thinking to himself before he types any further, says with a sigh, 'I'm having a hard time ending this'."

In short, what Charles Schulz has depicted for us through Snoopy is that many persons have a hard time trying to define what is a fulfilling life compared to what has transpired in their lives. When all is said, life seems like a disaster even in the midst of one's success and affluence. Do we really know what we want from life? Can we ever overcome unrest and incompleteness within ourselves? Do we have a sustainable purpose to energize and empower us?

In a conversation after church one Sunday, I was enjoying a cup of coffee with a former business executive who informed me that he had been forced to retire at the age of 58 when his company was sold to a competitor; he was no longer needed. I asked him, "How are you doing now?" "Fine. I'm happy to be liberated," he replied. "But are you fulfilled?", I asked "Yes," he said. "Fulfillment is being able to do what you want to do when you want to do it". But is that a satisfactory definition of fulfillment? "Of course, I have plenty to do. My morning is spent staying physically fit; my appointments begin at noon. I can spend more time now with my family and pay more attention to building my investment portfolio. In addition, I support a few philanthropic projects–which gives me pleasure."

"But do you still maintain a real sense of purpose in your life?" I asked.

"Well, that depends on what you mean by purpose. I no longer find myself dictated to by my business calendar.

I have more time to live outside the box of company structures and to be my own person, which I couldn't do earlier. In fact, I have been doing a better job of managing my investments than the bank did. I have time now to read *The Wall Street Journal.* I don't feel any obligation to volunteer my time to United Way, the Salvation Army or any of that good stuff, or for that matter even my church. Besides," he added, "I don't have any guilt feelings. I have more time for myself."

"But hasn't your lifestyle become more selfish than ever? Don't you feel you have some larger obligations to society?" And then without replying further, he said he was sorry, but had to leave for a Sunday luncheon date.

Life no doubt for some is moving quicker than anticipated. We need to admit that we never know what tomorrow might bring. Some may even remember that our sacred text says, "Come now, you who say, 'Today or tomorrow we will go to such and such a town and spend a year there, doing business and earning money and having fun.' Yet, we do not even know what tomorrow will bring." (James 4:13-14) Actually, what is the aim of our lives? Are we simply a mist that appears for a short time and then vanishes? This question is raised in James.

There are no guarantees on longevity. What's at stake on a daily basis is the enduring meaning of our lives. When and where will we find contentment? This is a major question facing us throughout our life's journey. As the Psalmist reminds us, *"We live for seventy years or so (with luck we might make it to eighty). And what do we have to show for it? Trouble...Toil and trouble and a marker in the graveyard."* (Psalm 90: 9-10 from Peterson's, *The Message.*))

It is within this context of reality that the Psalmist asks God to *"Teach us to count our days that we may gain a wise heart"* (Psalm 90:12). In other words, teach us, God, to live wisely and well. Many of us are living well, but are we living wisely? *The purpose-driven life must include more than one's self.* It is to offer one's self to God and to care for one another. In a special issue of *Time* (June 14, 2004, p. 48) honoring President Reagan, his wife Nancy writes, "Ronnie always believed that God has a plan for each of us and that we might not now know what it is now." The purpose-driven life of a believer is focused on pursuing with passion *the Divine Will rather than our wills throughout our lifetime.*

Truthfully, we all want to experience more fulfillment today rather than in the hereafter. Unfortunately, too many in our global society are seeking self-fulfillment without God. Some are among our neighbors, and others are family members and friends. It seems most of us only seek God's company in times of crisis. When we are forced to face reality, we find that there are no guarantees in life; tomorrow will bring whatever it will bring. That's why the Psalmist prays to God saying,

"Teach us to count our days that we may gain a wise heart". (Psalm 90:12)

Fulfillment is finding God at the center of your life on a daily basis. From the very start of our existence, we find ourselves searching for fulfillment. It's one of the first truths in the Bible. *We are created in the image of God!* Theologically referred to as *the imago Dei*, meaning we are shaped by God's Will, not ours. Believers have been taught through the centuries to faithfully practice this divine nature of caring in our relationships with one another *through acts of forgiving love.* The message of Jesus was to renew this relationship that had been tarnished for so long in our underlying histories and conflicted assumptions of human nature. The outreach of Jesus as God's son promotes an inclusive and harmonious spirit that affirms the *imago Dei* (God's image) manifested in our diverse cultures and contrasting lifestyles, but we have been unwilling to overcome these walls separating us.

Our essential wish has been to exert our desire and willpower over others, bypassing the enduring peace we claim publicly. While our means of warfare have improved over time, unfortunately our means for peacemaking hasn't. Today's essential distrust leads humankind in deadly pathways that defy the divine grace and mercy of our Creator-God. No single political ideology can guarantee universal peace and goodwill when distrust prevails. Haven't we had enough "great walls" and "towers of babble" in human history? Let's

55

wake up to a future that can unite us in security and mutual trust following God's Will, *instead of tribal wills pulling us apart.*

Are we afraid to grasp the Creator's purposes for our universal creation, allowing us to sidestep the egocentric gamesmanship of political leaders on all sides? All faiths have a calling to pray without ceasing, to discern the future wisely for humankind, seeking God's Will, not just individual desires. This was not God's intention for our creation. We are called upon to become goodwill ambassadors who can benefit one another, and together avoid the human pandemics known as world wars. God's Will for peace is far more global and universal than our border walls often dictated by economic incentives. God's horizon and perspective for peace are far ahead of us humans. In fact, God doesn't need a passport as we do.

We must realize what it means to be empowered in God's image for the glory of our Creator, not simply for ourselves. Have we lost the Big Picture of our faiths working together to advance the diversity inherent in God's Will, revealed in the *imago Dei,* directing us to tomorrow's world? Our economic battles of the past have contributed to our growing inequality worldwide which we have accepted in pious ways, forgetting that God doesn't really take sides in our trade deals. God hasn't any national passport. Poverty, however, increases throughout the world in the midst of our questionable economic battles.

We need to review Paul's epistle to us written from Rome:

"Take your everyday, ordinary life – your sleeping, eating, going-to-work, and walking-around life – and place it before God as an offering. Embracing what God does for you is the best thing you can do for him. Don't become so well- adjusted to your culture that you fit into it without even thinking. Instead, fix your attention on God. You'll be changed from the inside out. Readily recognize what he wants from you, and quickly respond to it. Unlike the culture around you, always dragging you down to its level of immaturity, God brings the best out of you, develops well-formed maturity in you." (Peterson's translation of Romans 12:1-2 in *The Message.)*

What overarching attitudes and reservations are we harboring that prevent us from designing a relevant biblical passport for today? What are we really afraid of currently that needs discussion in our circles of faith and public discourse? In short, what stage of spiritual maturity do we aspire to, as we discuss our economic concerns with the next generation? Will we have risk takers seeking *God's Will* instead of their self-interests?

Scripture to consider:
Psalm 90:12
Romans 12:1-2
James 4:13- 14
I John 4:9-5:3

Books and commentary for classroom and neighborhood discussion:

Hans Kung, *A Global Ethic for Global Politics and Economics,* Oxford University Press, UK.

Marilynne Robinson, *What Are We Doing Here?,* Farrar, Straus and Giroux, a volume of essays supporting America's egalitarian traditions and institutions. This timely book encourages citizens to find guidance in the confusion of political change. Her writings serve as a timely political theology with a biblical emphasis featuring kindness and generosity to support strangers beyond our shores, since we all are members of God's creation in the spirit of the *imago Dei.* In addition to national citizenship, the believer's ultimate citizenship is under one's Creator. As time moves on, we may realize internally that we have dual citizenship in heaven as well as on earth in keeping with our sacred texts. Why else would Congress support a national motto saying, **"In God We Trust"?** In addition, our public trust in God is included when pledging allegiance to the nation's flag. *Or are these pledges said in vain today?* Do Americans honestly trust in God as witnessed in our public and spiritual behavior? I find more spiritual doubt present today when trust in fellow citizens as well as God is questionable. Are true values reflected in laws for equality? Can we maintain dual citizenship to Country and God at the same time when expressing our motto and pledge? From my readings, it seems our founders sought freedom in these matters since they were largely divided between deists and traditional believers, agreeing simply that the new nation would not have a state religion, but rather allow its citizens the freedom of choice in matters of personal beliefs and convictions.

Would it be timely and nationally unifying for Congress to invite citizens to review our national affirmations of divine trust by forming a politically balanced Commission of Citizens to examine our nation's pledge and motto wherever our flag is on display, calling for affirmation? Can we be honest with ourselves? Would such congressional action awaken us to confront today's global ethics crisis that faces citizens around the world? How serious are we about wanting America to be great without expecting similar ethical standards of quality-greatness throughout our global society, if peace and justice are to have meaning in our inter- connected and interdependent post-pandemic world? To what extent do we all need global agreement on values, if mutual trust and prosperity is to be built? Such questions and concerns matter in a world where poverty, lawlessness and the lack of respect for human dignity prevails in our decade of displaced human lives. Have the hopes and cries of humankind become no more than cardboard dreams? Can we imagine how transformative our lives could be, if we truly lived in a global society of trusting relationships, promoting collective prosperity for all? The religions of this world ought to unite in supporting such efforts for the sake of our Creator-God in the spirit of the imago Dei divinely upheld in our sacred texts. Politically our biblical God is not capitalist, socialist, communist, etc. For that matter, without a national passport, God's love already encompasses the wonders of creation and its fruits, desiring that we all might all live in plenty, in the spirit of the spirit of the *imago Dei* fulfilling our common stewardship to our Creator-God.

God's global ethic is for everyone's mutual benefit and survival. It is not the monopoly of any single religion or nation. Anything else would be parochial and perhaps unsafe in an age of algorithms. See Hannah Fry's recent book, *Hello World: Being Human in the Age of Algorithms*. (W.W. Norton & Company) Believers with feelings of indifference will be held responsible for future apocalypses that might occur. Why are we waiting to acknowledge one another's calling in the *imago Dei?* God's Will welcomes us to live a fuller life. Embedded in the *imago Dei* we have a higher calling to be goodwill ambassadors (soulmates) to enrich lives in our lifetime.

Elizabeth Hinton, *"Turn Prison into Colleges", The New York Times,* March 6, 2018. While teaching as a visiting professor at Juniata College in Huntington, Pennsylvania years ago, I was invited by the nearby state maximum security prison to teach an experimental course on "Human Values" certified at Penn State University. I see merit in Dr. Hinton's prison idea.

Chapter 4. Surprising Realities

at Our Doorstep

Christmas is a time of surprises. Sometimes these surprises lie at our front doorstep. Let me briefly sketch five scenes I found at doorsteps.

Scene One

Some time ago, I was among the summer guest preachers at the Fifth Avenue Presbyterian Church in New York City. I arose early that Sunday to go jogging before the morning worship service. My hotel room was a few blocks from the church, as I ran by I noticed a homeless man asleep on the doorstep. This gave me an uneasy feeling knowing that I would be the guest preacher within a few hours facing a well-educated congregation traditionally dressed for a Sunday morning worship service. The reality of a homeless person sleeping on the church doorstep can be repeated in Pittsburgh, Chicago, Los Angeles as well as New York City and almost any city in the world.

Scene Two

I was walking to an early-morning breakfast meeting in downtown Pittsburgh with pastors and business leaders at the First Presbyterian Church; I saw a copy of *The Wall Street Journal on the church's doorstep.* I don't know why, but I found myself surprised and amused. Evidently someone on that church's staff was staying well informed on the economic realities of our business culture. Without money, none of our institutions and businesses, whether profit or non-profit, would be able to survive. Money is important, but unfortunately it seems we worry over income distribution rather than income creation. The preoccupation of today's church with decreasing contributions and loss of members highlights this factor over and over again. Fund raising for charities, education and religious causes isn't an easy task; we would rather pay others to do it for us professionally and often find ourselves dissatisfied with the results. Where have all the generous givers gone? Are they mostly found among the past generation of givers? Will we be able to continue the learning and medical standards required for future generations? Will a forthcoming generation experience improved standard for living as enjoyed by many of their parents and grandparents? Will we be able to afford spiritual centers in space to gather travelers together for fellowship and worship during significant times of major change requiring an unofficial ambassador of goodwill with wisdom?

Scene Three
My son Philip sent me a series of articles past and present from *The New Yorker* highlighting the life of Jesse Jackson. In the articles, Jesse recalled his boyhood days and how discouraged and depressed his father was. Things were not going well for the family financially. It was Christmas season, and there would be no exchanging of gifts in the family, and the food supply was low. Knowing it was Christmas Eve, Jesse's mother said, "We can at least go and add to the congregation".

When the Jackson family returned from church, there were six bags of groceries sitting on their front doorstep. Jackson's family felt the delivery man had made some mistake. As Jesse tells it, "We were all sure somebody would call for them. We took the groceries inside and waited. We waited two entire days, and nobody called for the food stuff. Finally, a Mr. Dave drove by and asked if we had gotten his order. Momma said, "Oh, yes, we weren't sure exactly who they were for, but we have been holding them for you."

He answered, "They're for you-all. Just a little something I wanted to do after all the help you have been to me for so long."

Mr. Dave was elderly and wasn't able to leave any kind of written note. When Mr. Dave said, "I thought you-all, would just know," Jesse's mother started crying. The realities of hunger, joblessness and illiteracy were intertwined in that moment around those bags of grocery goods on the doorstep of the Jackson home.

Scene Four

Some years ago, Pittsburgh experienced a lack of daily newspapers for nearly eight months. This taught households and businesses many lessons. While it was interesting to learn that we could all survive without the daily paper, I have to admit, that I missed my morning paper. Since then, frankly, I haven't taken my morning newspaper for granted. The newspaper strike illustrated realistically the pressures for change and its consequences for labor, management and readers alike. While we still have a number of smaller newspapers today, only one dominant newspaper serves the majority of the local population known as *The Pittsburgh Post-Gazette.* While we realize in our reflective moments that life without changes is unreal, we nevertheless still have our dis-ease with change caused by many sources including "social viruses" too.

Every change brings pluses and minuses, with reactions and protests, reflecting personal and collective self-interest. We know that change in our midst is inevitable. We have gone from stagecoaches to Model T's, to newer American and foreign automobiles, and now to Uber drivers and an upcoming generation of driverless cars. Artificial intelligence is growing rapidly with many consequences, fears and serious impact upon labor, management and consumers.

Holding onto the past with nostalgia is neither realistic nor farsighted. Any nation seeking to be first in the world is also in danger of becoming an anachronism under increasing pressure and pace of change. Future years will be evaluated from the perspective of rapid change according to theoretical physicists like Michio Kaku in his latest book, *The Future of Humanity* (Doubleday). Will Kaku's insights stimulate our thinking as did the late Stephen Hawking's forecasting did in recent decades?

We need to look beyond today's **"generation games"** according to research scholar John Quiggin of the University of Queensland who writes that, *"'Millennial' Means Nothing", (The New York Times*, February 2018). Today's younger generations require greater stimulation beyond the cultural and religious wars of yesterday; future change is related to tomorrow's explorations. For example, to deny climate warming today is myopic. Meaningful success is determined by how willing we are to navigate through the politics of climate change to discover passageways of hope not yet explored. Knowledgeable persons are calling us to take action in preparing for our next major pandemic on the horizon.

In 1963, a Louisiana State University business professor, Leon C. Megginson, was invited to speak at the convention of the Southwestern Social Science Association of researchers. His remarks were published in the quarterly journal of the Association. The central idea of his remarks centered on Charles Darwin's *"On the Origin of Species"*. Megginson did not use any quotation marks from Darwin and apparently his phrasing was repetitive. No doubt he was influenced by the methodology used in Darwin's research which was published and distributed in 1859. Professor Megginson's reflections were astute and insightful for the audience of scholars present: *"Yes, change is the basic law of nature. But (it seems) the changes wrought by the passage of time affect individuals and institutions in different ways. According to Darwin's reflection On the Origin Of Species, 'It is not the most intellectual of the species that survives; nor is it the strongest of the species that survives; but (rather) the species that survives is the one best able to adapt and adjust to the changing environment in which it finds itself.'* Applying this theoretical concept to us today as individuals, implies that the civilization that is able to survive is the (one) most able to adapt (creatively) to changes-- physical, social, political, moral, spiritual & environmental which confronts us."

How willing are we to accept changing attitudes once considered sacred? Perhaps change among all living relationships and species serves as a useful reminder of our interconnectedness—Divine and human—as we reclaim our stewardship responsibilities to creation as our Creator-God intended since the beginning of time.

Was this biblical understanding part of the theme behind the Oscar-winning film of 2018, *"The Shape of Water" with new life in an underwater world!* Undergoing change within our species will play a significant role in advancing our interconnected lives. How much weight do we place on God's creativity to ignite our imagination today? How large a role ought our God play in today's modern world preoccupied with a list of innovations needed? Have we established an adequate and creative means of addressing past and future religious tensions when asked by enquiring believers and non-believers seeking greater relevance and direction to nurture their lives and communities? If past efforts are insufficient, let's consider a new *Global Center for Religious Understanding & Cooperation* that includes courses and research projects for faculty, students, trustees and international scholars & clergy. Such a Center would draw colleges, universities, divinity schools and seminaries into creative partnerships with common interests in a changing world. This may also be a wise way to educate tomorrow's goodwill ambassadors into the program in our internet and interdisciplinary age, creating innovative interfaith projects that highlight our common stewardship under our Creator-God, advancing *the spirit of the imago* **Dei** in our global society where human suffering affects anyone anywhere.

Perhaps a modern type of a good Samaritan is evident in Charles Chen Yidan, founder of the Tencent Charity Foundation, presently supporting scholars and researchers globally to advance data-based evidence in the social and physical sciences that truly improves the quality of human lives. Hopefully, the Tencent Charity Foundation in their goodwill efforts will offer the *Yidan Prize* to all the known *helping professions* that could enhance ethical and spiritual relationships among humankind locally and globally.

This changing world is widening our vision to do more good than we have presently envisioned in the unfortunate winner-take-all climate of today that promotes a war-like atmosphere in global affairs. This distrustful climate is not in the best interests of humankind. *Major wars no longer serve the best interest of nations large and small.* Such comments may seem unrealistic to yesterday's strategists and dictators with their democratic façades backed by an authoritarian spirit that dishonors human life and the significance of true freedom, the very backbone of true democracy. It is this spirit of freedom that keeps human life human embedded in our *imago Dei*, which is sacred to our biblical history created as we are to be free in our worship with respect for one another's humanity under God. (Deuteronomy 30:19-20; Micah 3:5-6; and Ecclesiastes 7:15-18) In short, the chief aim of humankind is to restore ourselves collectively as a trusting global community that upholds our diversity through essential institutions of governance, health care, education, an honest marketplace, and international trade that enables all parties to succeed within the roots of the *imago Dei* in our respective lives. A zero-sum philosophy of life is the wrong road to take. Higher rewards at the mountain top-- peace, justice and goodwill-- require wisdom and humility to avoid the tempting trade-offs we will later regret.

Scene Five

The discovery of God's grace appeared for me many years ago. I was in the 3rd Grade; it was a difficult period for our family. Perhaps it was not as bad as Jesse Jackson experienced, but I knew it was a hard time with gloom and despair at home. And Christmas was coming. One day on my return from elementary school, I discovered a large package at our front doorstep. "Mommy," I called out, "Were you expecting something?" "No," she answered. There was not a single mark of identification on the package. No neighbors responded to our inquiries. Finally, my parents opened the package. It was a large Bible, the kind you would find on the pulpit or lectern of a church. However, there was no indication as to the source. We shared the news with neighbors, and no one claimed it. Reluctantly, in our simple faith we accepted that large Bible as a gift from God – a sign of hope at that moment. We saw ourselves as precious before God, regardless of the odds against us. God was not going to forsake us no matter how tough our lives seemed. We were special and sanctified in God's sight. We read from the Bible that day of how God cared for us as the lilies of the field and even more. This scriptural affirmation lifted our family spirit and placed our situation into perspective.

These five doorstep scenes each illustrate basic human needs and the realities of God's grace. To begin with, we all have need for survival and safety. The homeless man sleeping on the church doorstep, the bags of grocery goods at the Jesse Jackson home testify to these human realities. The hurricanes in the south and the flood waters in the Midwest have spoken to many of us as we reached into our pockets to contribute funds. Even more tragic for us are the television scenes of starving Somalians, Syrians and others in their strife-torn countries. Survival and safety are universal needs, and none of us are exempt. The question is how generous are we in assisting neighbors and strangers through these realities?

We often draw a narrow circle of concern around family and friends, neglecting the survival and safety needs of strangers. When do we respond generously beyond rationalizations that back our tribal biases and concern for personal security? I recently heard the claim, "The only charity that I practice is with my family–period!"

Does the Bible teach that charity begins and also ends at home? Will we raise such questions as we discuss our biblical passports with our diverse backgrounds? The scene with *The Wall Street Journal* on the church's doorstep illustrates not only the economic conditions of a marketplace culture, but also the realities of a business-driven world that seemingly divides itself between winners and losers. To understand the context of our culture is to embrace the fact that while we are congratulating one party, we are also commiserating with another. Competition seems to be at the essence of our lifestyle. Corporations are tolerated as long as they profitably support the sports team, nation, university or business self-interest. Corporations at times are downgraded when personal ambition or even national security interferes. *The Wall Street Journal* with its front-page stories illustrates that trade-offs are integral in a win/lose culture. The question is always how high a price are we willing to pay in order to win? What trade-offs are we willing to make and can afford? How much of a gambler do we choose to be? Are there limits to the price we will pay for one another's soul? How transparent are we in confronting God and one another? In the end, what matters most?

Mr. Dave in Jesse Jackson's story was doing more than helping the Jackson family to survive. With his gift of groceries, he was actually fulfilling his own need to share and fulfill his reason for being. Mr. Dave was meeting his own concern to articulate his search for holiness, his need to be closer to God's embrace. We need to grasp the words found in Matthew's story of good news that offers a divine perspective for a lifetime of journeys among humankind that includes us as well.

"Consider the lilies of the field, how they grow", says Jesus to his followers: "They neither toil nor spin. Yet I tell you, even Solomon in all of his glory was not clothed like one of these. But if God so clothes the grass

71

of the field which is alive today and tomorrow is thrown into the oven, will he not much more clothe you – you of little faith. Therefore, do not worry, saying, "What will we eat?" or "What will we drink?" or "What will we wear?" For it is the Gentiles who strive for all these things: And indeed, your heavenly father knows that you need all these things. But strive first for the kingdom of God and his righteousness, and all these things will be given to you as well. So do not worry about tomorrow, for tomorrow will bring worries of its own. Today's trouble is enough for today." (Matthew 6: 25-34)

The Bible at our family doorstep has reminded me through the years to look beyond the anguish and anxieties of present circumstances to an abiding reality –- namely, Gods faithfulness and willingness to uphold us daily. "Do not be anxious about tomorrow for tomorrow will be anxious for itself." What kind of comfort will tomorrow's goodwill ambassador provide when discussing his biblical passport with others?

Scripture to consider:
Genesis 1:26-27
Micah 7:7-20
Matthew 4:4, 6:9-34
I Corinthians 3:16-17
Philippians 3:3-10

Books and articles for classroom and neighborhood discussions:

Jon Meacham, *The Soul of America: The Battle for our Better Angels,* Random House, is one of his recent contribution with a discussion on American values.

Sharon Watkins, *Power Failure,* Crown Business, writes on the ethical downfall of Enron, during the leadership of Kenneth L. Lay and Jeffrey K. Skilling. Watkins was an accounting executive at Enron and lost her position after choosing to be a whistleblower. Following the publication of her book (2004), she lectured at Pittsburgh Seminary's Center on Business, Religion & Public Life which was well attended by seminarians, graduate business students and faculties located near the Seminary.

Steven Levingston, **Kennedy** *And King: The President, the Pastor, and the Battle Over Civil Rights*, Hachette Books, New York. Levingston's book describes the difficult process of engagement during the civil rights struggle between leading politicians and activists, with King seeking common ground that later led to President Lyndon Johnson's signature on the Civil Rights Act of 1964 as the law of the land. Levingston reminds us of King's comment about Kennedy, "It is a difficult thing to teach a president".

Rushworth M. Kidder, *How Good People Make Tough Choices: Resolving the Dilemmas of Ethical Living,* William Morrow and Company, Inc., New York

Kelly James Clark (editor), *Philosophers Who Believe: The Spiritual Journeys of 11 Leading Thinkers,* Inter-Varsity Press, Downers Grove, Illinois

Phil Knight, *Shoe DOG: A Memoir by the Creator of Nike,* Scribner, New York If you are discussing his book in Oregon, invite Knight to be your guest.

Terra Brockman, *"Trash to Table: A feast of food scraps", The Christian Century,* January 17, 2017. How many Americans realize that we throw away almost as much food as we eat? The authors present a useful idea for ambassadors of goodwill to remember on future assignments.

David Brooks, *"Worthy Is the Lamb",* on the changing realities of contemporary politics in the United States, *The New York Times,* March 16, 2018.

Nitsuh Abebe, *"Apocalypse Now", The New York Times Magazine,* September 8, 2017. offers an explanation of apocalypse as we face the existential threat of climate change confronting humankind. Will we have a common viewpoint to unite us as we wisely prepare to avoid such a costly crisis?

Nicholas Kristof, *"A Parable of Self-Destruction"*, reflections on Easter Island in the South Pacific, *The New York Times,* March 18, 2018

Yousaf Butt*, "Avoiding Traffic Pileups In Outer Space", The New York Times,* March 20, 2018. Butt is an astrophysicist and was associated with the Office of Space and Advance Technology at the State Department.

Miroslav Volf and Matthew Croasmun, *"Universal yet particular: A Christian vision of flourishing for all", The Christian Century,* February 13, 2019 --adapted from their recent book, *For the Life of the World: Theology That Makes a Difference.* The co-authors teach at the Yale University Center for Faith and Culture.

Part II: Treat Individuals as Sacred

Chapter 5. Building Trusting Relationships

Everyone appreciates genuine relationships of trust. Surveys indicate that in the sixties, 58% of Americans believed "most people" could be trusted. A survey three decades later – in the Nineties – reported that the trust factor had fallen to 37%. More recently, we see further loss of trust within families, communities and organizations. According to leadership expert Dr. Michael Maccoby, loyalty and trust in organizations are diminished, causing anxiety over safety at work and salary differentials. Trust disappears as individuals place their self and village interests ahead of national and global interests. We are creating new walls of separation in an interconnected world, neglecting the standards of trust envisioned by our Creator's gift of the *imago Dei*, God's image embedded in us.

Trust in God is the cornerstone for trusting one another. We need to recover the biblical link between human trust and divine trust. Truth-telling and forgiving love are requisites in relationships with God and with one another. As a nation we claim, "In God We Trust," but in our daily lives that seems to be an empty motto, our trust in God depends usually on the outcome, otherwise we feel alone and dis-empowered in our relationships within the community. Efforts to build human trust by other means are unsustainable unless nurtured and linked to forgiving love that cares and heals yesterday's brokenness as we envision a new horizon with emerging relationships that matter. Each person is divinely endowed with the capacity to forgive and to rebuild cornerstones of trust that endure.

Trust is not a science; it is not even an art. Trust is an experience, whether in person, online, or through cell phones. Trust calls for risk-taking within the weight of broken relationships and lost purposes. The dynamics inherent in forgiving is never easy. As we encourage openness, we bolster our willingness to participate as risk-takers, implementing the fragile roots of trust building. God has destined us to belong to one another, calling us to be a healing and trusting community of imperfect persons. Religious congregations have their share of imperfect followers and leaders whatever their faith might be.

Implied in the very nature of trust also lies the reality of betrayal. We need to be as realistic as Jesus who singled out Simon Peter, his outspoken disciple, predicting that Peter would deny him three times before the early morning call of the rooster. When Peter recalled the prediction, he cried in shame. The betrayal reminded

Peter of his vulnerability. His future ministry was influenced by that betraying moment as he taught and practiced forgiving love among the growing number of believers. Peter was energized by the divine forgiveness seen in Jesus, which encouraged him to rebuild broken relationships as the community of believers continued to increase in number. The rooster (rather than the cross) is placed on the steeple of some churches (including Pittsburgh Seminary) as a reminder of Peter's vulnerability and God's redeeming grace that encourages and beckons us to trust and forgive, authentic forgiveness never ends. It entails a painful process of truth-telling so essential in leading us to healthier relationships with one another. Trusting God and each other is not a static affair; neither is it to be taken for granted. There is always a price to be paid, oftentimes requiring restitution from both sides.

Types of Trust

This biblical standard of trust needs to be distinguished from other types of trust. For instance, there is ***simple trust*** mentioned in a book co-authored by Robert C. Solomon and Fernando Flores, *Building Trust: in Business, Politics, Relationships and Life*, Oxford University Press. **Simple trust** begins in human infancy. but fails to mature when life becomes more complicated. Simple trust is characterized by a certain innocence, often shocked by painful betrayals.

Simple trust often gives way to cynicism or skepticism, leading to the practice of *cordial hypocrisy*. This attitude often permeates social gatherings and encounters. In cordial hypocrisy, the distinction between etiquette and ethics becomes confused; lying becomes acceptable and normative. Of course, this leads to limited trust within encounters. We seek authentic colleagues and friends who listen before offering quick advice concerning injured relationships.

As we move from simple trust and its consequences, we long for a more meaningful level of trust. Lives are clearly diminished if we do not belong to some network of trusting relationships. Religious congregations, sports teams, clubs, etc. can offer networks for trust-building. Every network of trust requires a willingness to listen well, to be honest and to respond to the situation wisely. Such sharing can actually be a lesson in vulnerability, with a willingness to learn from one another. We can't be pushed into this relationship; we need to respect one another's freedom for privacy and practice the necessary sensitivity that suspends judgment. Like Jesus, we need to listen carefully to strangers, as he did with the woman at the well, accepting her without hasty judgement. Such an approach will take us beyond *simple trust to critical trust*, a level of discernment leading both sides to show respect. Each time we engage in trust, we are also taking a risk. God is certainly aware of the risks in the history of humankind. A negative experience can be devastating, but disengagement can lead to despair. Life without trusting relationships is lonely; it undermines our spiritual and emotional health. One of God's most fulfilling gifts is the experience of authentic trusting relationships, Divine and earthly as we journey through life in fellowship reflecting *the spirit of the imago Dei embedded in faith, hope and love.*

Finally, there will be those unwilling to engage in this tough process leading to *authentic trust.* Some will opt for *blind trust* – a fool's paradise. Blind trust should not be confused with faith or "the leap of faith" as expressed in religious literature. *Blind trust* is an expression of denial, an attempt to bury past hurts and betrayals. Such a journey of self-deception and false trust often abounds. Communities of *blind trust* have fixed expectations and rules within a restrictive atmosphere of empty promises, false security and personal loss of freedom. Jonestown and the Branch Davidians are tragic examples of *blind trust* given to leaders and by their followers. *Blind trust* does not lead to a more fulfilling life.

In summary, simple trust can be unrealistic in the midst of today's complexity. *Blind trust* denies us freedom and is ultimately self-deceptive. Critical and discerning trust is rooted in having true relationships with God and one another as witnessed in the lives of Abraham and Sarah and their descendants. Authentic trust has its realism and is redemptive. It addresses our disappointments and betrayals, healing us from yesterday's broken promises, and prepares us to take risks again propelled by the biblical examples of divine forgiveness and its power to restore relationships even today. The scars from the past remind us that it is time to move on, to be liberated from the demons of distrust, and to uncover genuine trust to renewed lives and communities.

Scripture to consider:
Ruth chapters 1-4
Psalm 37 & 139
Proverbs 3:1-8; 31: 1-31 & 29:18 ("Where there is no vision, the people perish.")
Ecclesiastes 5
Matthew 26:30-35; 69-75
Leviticus 19: 33-34 (Reminds us that the Israelites were once aliens in the land of Egypt, while today's global citizens could become tomorrow's aliens facing a planetary civilization in a space war hoping for peace someday.

Books and articles for classroom and neighborhood discussions:

David Goldfield, *The Gifted Generation: When Government Was Good,* Bloomsbury, 2017, New York highlights the importance of building responsible government to gain the people's trust.

Yuval Noah Harari, *Sapiens: A Brief History of Humankind,* Vintage Books, U.K.

David Brooks, *"Democracy Is A Way of Life"*, *The New York Times,* 2/16//2018

Casey Cep, *"Without A Prayer"*, *The New Yorker,* October 29, 2018. Her article explains the mistrust among Americans who claim atheism as their faith. Or is there a neglected fear among us to discuss our doubts?

Raffi Khatchadourian, *"A Century of Silence: A Family Survives the Armenian Genocide and Its Long Aftermath"*, *The New Yorker,* January 5, 2015. This staff writer for *The New Yorker* relates his Armenian heritage traced back to the Armenian Genocide and his ancestry in the Middle East. There is much written on genocides today, including, Benny Morris and Dror Zéevi's, *"The Thirty-Year Genocide: Turkey's Destruction of Its Christian Minorities, 1894-1924,* Harvard University Press, Boston

Peter W. Marty, *"Zero-sum living"*. *From the Publisher of The Christian Century,* July 3, 2019. Marty points out, "Zero-sum thinking fosters a logic of scarcity— 'What will I have left?'" Not the best way to have any kind of fruitful relationships.

Chapter 6. Changeless Commitments in a Changing World

We have been educated in the School of Hard Knocks. Some refer to it as the School of Experience or the School of Reality. Whatever name we use, it is the one school from which we never graduate. We were enrolled at birth and graduate at death. The curriculum consists of case studies from our experiences. The basic course at the School of Hard Knocks is referred to as *Life 101*. The simple reality often overlooked, is that *this basic course* requires a lifetime of attendance whatever our profession or challenges might be confronting us.

The lessons learned in Life 101 may actually raise more questions than answers. Here is a brief sampling:

1. Why isn't life fair?
2. Why are we so suspicious and mistrusting of one another?
3. If money talks, why can't we buy lasting health, true love and friendships?

4. If winning isn't everything, why is it we feel so terrible when we lose?

5. If it is true that nothing fails like success, why do we keep desiring success?

6. Why do we find greed rather than generosity in our encounters with others?

7. Why are egos never satisfied? Are there any perfect fair deals?

8. Why are there so many unexplained tragedies in life?

9. Who is responsible for evil? Or do bad things just happen?

10. Why is it that even good people do bad things?

There are, of course, many more questions in Life 101. Our learning institutions (churches, seminaries, universities, etc.) seek to bring a faith or reasoned perspective to these questions, while courses in sociology, psychology, biology, economics and the sciences also seek explanations. At times we realize that the way we see the problem may be the problem in our quest for answers.

Two basic observations surface in Life 101: first, that change is inevitable. According to the author and psychotherapist, Rollo May, "Change is a great word in America; we not only believe in it – we worship it" *(The Cry for Myth)*. Just look at our fashion industry, automotive styling, personnel turnover in any organization, or the implications of cyberspace, and we see that change is inevitable. The Greek philosopher

Heraclitus went so far as to say, "Nothing endures but change." We celebrate lengthy anniversaries even as we are willing to accept change and reach for higher standards of expectation embedded as we are in our spiritual DNA *(the imago Dei)*.

In recent decades we have become aware of exciting social changes and breathtaking innovations reshaping our global expectations with hope and anxiety as we observe the overthrow of the old for the new. In the midst of all these changes, the cloud of 9/11 hangs over us and distorts our sense of discernment in planning for the future. According to cartographers in the U.S. State Department, world maps have seen more changes in recent decades than in the last 50 plus years. Nothing seems to be lasting in human affairs nationally or internationally.

Death also witnesses the inevitability of change. Everyone has his or her date with death. For some it is tragic and unexpected; for others it is an end to a long-life span. William S. Paley, the founder and builder of CBS, was a wealthy and powerful individual. Paley is quoted in his biography, *In All His Glory* by Sally Bedell Smith asking the question at age 89, *"Why do I have to die?"* In other words, why am I forced to change my status when it is against my will? Apparently, neither power, prestige nor money could buy off death or prevent change for Mr. Paley. Death is change, and it is inevitable. No one is exempt.

The second lesson that Life 101 teaches is that living without purpose is unsatisfying. It has been said that purposeful living is at the heart of keeping our vital signs alive. And where do we find this purpose? It's embedded in our commitments that give meaning to our lives. Are we able to live a purposeful life without commitments? Can there be meaningful commitments that outlast change? If change is inevitable, are commitments short-lived and victimized by change? Does change rob us of purpose or are there changeless commitments that endure? Does rapid change pervert us from enjoying a culture of commitment with loved ones?

For example, hardliners in the East and West who believed that the Cold War would never end, have been disillusioned with the results. They are now building political strength in forced forms of pseudo-democracy and pseudo-capitalism, denying citizens freedom of expression in a search to erase all traces of restrictive governance, that kills creativity and political expression.

As we circle the universe, we look for changeless commitments in this changing world to keep our life juices stirring within us. Most of us desire a zest and purpose for living, convinced in our very psyche that a truly fulfilled and satisfying life demands commitment to an abiding purpose. Without purpose, some have slipped into retirement early without excitement and enthusiasm, denying the pursuit of creative possibilities within us.

We need to review our commitments or lack of them. The quality or void in life is related to commitments or their absence. No one can be a whole person without meaningful and nourishing commitments. The revealing question in life isn't whether or not to commit, but rather to whom and to what.

What presently is our central driving force in life? Where will we be if the situation changes? For instance, is the center right now our life partner, our children, the nation, possessions, work or pleasure? Is it friends, church, school, a current project? What is at the center of life right at this moment? What is *the commitment* that gives meaning and zest for living?

If the center is one's spouse, what happens then if that spouse dies or leaves us? What if our nation is wrong, our family grows up, our possessions are stolen, our friends disappoint us, the church, school, business or cause espouse fails? Have we viewed the center of our existence wisely?

Paul's clear message in Romans 8 seeks to give perspective. God has provided a purpose for each of us. God is for us. The death and resurrection of Jesus the Christ is sufficient evidence of that for the Apostle Paul. Everything can change in life, says Paul. However, this changeless, core commitment from God is focused in

91

divine love exemplified in Jesus and continues to speak volumes to believers today. Thus, Paul urges us to also follow suit; to make Jesus the central core commitment of our lives. *The Center of all centers is the Jesus of Easter.* The resurrected Christ is the anchor that affirms and validates our destiny, and supports our values nurtured in faith, hope and love, keeping human life human. It is this life-giving commitment of Jesus that testifies to the enduring love of God that bears witness to believers so that we live from grace to grace, from mercy to mercy each day of our lives. Everyone's faith ought to have a *core meaning* that gives us hope.

Paul's sacred text in the *Epistle of Romans* declares that we can live with change and all its consequences if we are committed with heart, mind and soul to this changeless core of beliefs anchored in the Christ of faith, the Jesus of history:

> *If God is for us, who is against us? Who is to condemn? Who will separate us from the love of Jesus the Christ? Will hardship, distress, persecution, famine, nakedness, peril or sword? No, in all these things we are more than conquerors through Him who loved us. For I am convinced that neither death, nor life, nor angels, nor ruler, nor things present, nor things to come, nor powers, nor height, nor depth, nor anything else in all creation, will be able to separate us from the love of God in Jesus Christ our Lord.*

Romans8:31-39. (Peterson's translation, The Message)

Kent M. Keith a businessman and educator, was influenced I believe by the Apostle Paul's deep sense of commitment along with his own observations on life as expressed in his modest book, *"Anyway: The Paradoxical Commandments"* published by Berkley Books:

> *People are unreasonable, illogical, self-centered.*
> **Love them, anyway.**

> *If you do good, people will accuse you of selfish, ulterior motives.*
> **Do good, anyway.**

> *If you are successful, you will win false friends and true enemies.*
> **Do good, anyway**

> *The good you do today will be forgotten tomorrow.*
> **Do it, anyway.**

> *Honesty and frankness make you vulnerable.*
> **Be honest and frank, anyway.**

> *The biggest men and women with the biggest ideas can be shot down by the smallest men and women with the smallest minds.*

Think big, anyway.

People favor underdogs, but I notice they follow the top dogs.
Fight for some underdogs, anyway.

What you spend years building may be destroyed overnight.
Build, anyway.

People really need help, but they may attack you if you help them.
Try to help people, anyway.

Give the world the best you have, and you'll get kicked in the teeth.
Give the world the best you have, anyway.

As we each review our commitments, how changeless are they in this changing world? Life is filled with zest and purpose through lasting commitments. Why do we keep on resisting the spiritual realities of our underlying unity in *the imago Dei?* Can we afford to admit our broken relations, with our newly designed biblical passports in hand? Are we willing to step out and begin anew by God's grace, in spite of our contradictory acts? This is our situation today as we try prayerfully to approach one another. No wonder we find it difficult at times to become goodwill ambassadors directing a positive impact on humankind as we cross political and religious borders. We have our self-made gated communities of hypocrisy that need to open up to authentic fellowship as our Creator intended, for us to live in *the spirit of the imago Dei.*

Scripture to consider:
Genesis chapters 6, 7, 8, & 9 (stories on Noah and his sons)
Psalm 70, 71, 72 & 145 (God's unsearchable greatness and generosity)
Romans 8: 31-39
Colossians 3 & 4
1 John, 2 John, & 3 John
Jude verses 1-25

Books, articles and films for classroom and neighborhood discussions:
Margot Lee Shetterly, *Hidden Figures,* William Morrow, New York. Shetterly's true story has enlightened us to changing societies.

Randall Fuller, *The Book That Changed America: How Darwin's Theory of Evolution Ignited a Nation,* Viking, N Y. Charles Darwin left us with many unforgettable statements and observations that require wider discussion among faith traditions. Darwin's research indicated that, *"It is not the strongest of the species that survive, nor the most intelligent, but the one most responsive to change."* Professor Fuller is a faculty member at the University of Kansas.

Nancy Koehn, *Forged in Crisis: The Power of Courageous Leadership In Turbulent Times,* Scribner, New York

Four films to discuss: Martin Doblmeier documentary, *The Power of Forgiveness* on the Amish school killing; the life of German theologian *Dietrich Bonhoeffer;* the *"USS Indianapolis: Men of Courage"*; and a film on the Scottish Olympian, Eric Liddel in China, *"On Eagle's Wing.*

The **Rand Corporation's** *Rand Review,* March-APRIL 2018, offered insights from Francis Fukuyama, Michael D. Rich, and Soledad O'Brien on the theme, *"The Perils of Truth Decay Today". Truth Decay* is composed by four trends in society carrying a negative impact on the quality of our thinking as a global society. *First* is the heightened "disagreement about facts and analytical interpretation of data". *Second,* we find ourselves out of focus between what is an opinion and what is fact. *Third,* we have increased the "volume and influence of opinion and personal experience across the communication landscape". *Fourth,* the combined result of the above three points has diminished trust in outstanding respected institutions.

Chapter 7. Making Ethical Decisions That Matter

King Solomon was guided by the statutes of his father David; he was known to offer incense and sacrifices at high places principally at Gibeon countless times. "At Gibeon, the Lord appeared to Solomon in a dream by night, and said, 'Ask what I shall give you.' Solomon answered, 'You have shown great and steadfast love to your servant David my father, because he walked before you in faithfulness, in righteousness and in uprightness of heart toward you; and you have kept for him this great and steadfast love, and have given him a son to sit on his throne today. And now, O Lord my God, you have made your servant king in place of my father David, although I am only a little child; I do not know how to go out or come in.

And your servant is in the midst of the people whom you have chosen, a great people, so numerous they cannot be numbered or counted. *Give your servant therefore an understanding mind to govern your people, able to discern between good and evil; for who can govern your great people?'" (I Kings 3: 3-9)*

It pleased the Lord that Solomon had asked. "God said to him, 'Because you have asked this and have not asked for yourself long life or riches or for the life of your enemies but have asked for yourself understanding *to discern what is right.* I now do according to your word. Indeed, I give you a wise and discerning mind, so that none like you has been before you and none like you shall arise after you. I give you also what you have not asked, both riches and honor, so that no other king shall compare with you. If you will walk in my ways, keeping my statues and my commandments, as your father David walked, then I will lengthen your life.'" (I Kings 3: 10-14)

It appears that Solomon then awoke from his conversation with God, accepting his dialogue with God as a significant dream. He then went to Jerusalem where he stood before the ark of the covenant of the Lord. Here he offered burnt offerings and offerings of well-being as he provided a feast for all his servants. (I Kings 3:15)

As mentioned earlier, two women approached the king to determine which was the true mother of a given child. One woman claimed, "Please, my lord, this woman and I live in the same house; and I gave birth while she was in the house. Then on the third day after I gave birth; this woman also gave birth. We were together; there was no one else with us in the house, only the two of us were in the house. Then this woman's son died in the night, because she lay on him. She got up in the middle of the night and took my son lying beside me while your servant slept. She laid him at her breast and laid her dead son at my breast. When I rose in the morning to nurse my son, I saw that he was dead; but when I looked at him closely in the morning, clearly it was not the son I had borne." But the other woman said, "No, the living son is mine, and the dead son is yours." The first said, "No, the dead son is yours. and the living son is mine." So, they argued before the king. (I Kings 3: 16-22)

Then the king said, "The one says, 'This is my son that is alive, and your son is dead,' while the other says, 'Not so! Your son is dead, and my son is the living one.'" So, the king said, *"Bring me a sword," and they brought a sword before the king. The king said, "Divide the living boy in two; then give half to the one, and half to the other."* But the woman whose son was alive, said to the king—because compassion for her son burned within her— "Please, my lord, give her the living boy; certainly, do not kill him!" The other said, "It shall be neither mine nor yours; divide it". Then the king responded; "Give the first woman the living boy; do not kill him. *She is his mother."* And Israel heard of the judgment that the king had rendered; and they stood in awe of the king, because they perceived that the wisdom of God was in him, to execute justice. (I Kings 3: 23-28)

Election Day here and among most nations involves decision-making for citizens that adhere to some form of democratic governance for the sake of the nation's well-being and future. Choosing leaders is an important matter and can be difficult, even confusing for citizens who have the responsibility of voting. But all leaders (in whatever election process) also realize that voters may not find the outcome to their liking. Such feelings are similar in family decisions as well. Some aspect of authority is present at almost all stages of our lives from choosing our wardrobe, planning careers, and even choosing life partners. These choices can be difficult as we consider priorities, values, local rituals and cultural issues tied to traditions that may cause unrest.

Does your community have difficulty making decisions? Many do, especially on issues that affect the livelihood and education of family members. Will our sacred texts give us guidance? Whatever our faith tradition, we usually seek some measure of spiritual wisdom to intervene. This was seen in the divine promise made to King Solomon, delighting his people that their leader was divinely vested to make wise decisions on their behalf. As a leader Solomon's efforts were constantly under pressure demonstrating his understanding of justice under God.

Wisdom is more than an accumulation of knowledge, logic or even common sense. Wise decisions extend beyond our immediate comprehension of the situation and may appear for the moment nonsensical from a finite perspective. Praying for divine wisdom is actually *asking for the gift of divine hindsight before the event, which could imply a challenge to the status quo in resolving a crisis within the community with consequences.* King Solomon's judgment was always on trial. He sought authentic truth in the trial of the two women. Exercising wisdom is much more than yielding to popular pressure; young King Solomon was aware of this. Ethical decisions are usually a complex matter with legal, ethical, religious, economic and national factors co-mingling in the search for an acceptable resolution. Ethical decisions in political and financial affairs are also not easy, affecting lives and communities for generations to come.

Solomon was aware of this factor. Was he ready to divide the infant in two? The stakes were high; the king was gambling his reputation as well as the future of the child. Was the king's thinking process in error? Was he manipulating the two mothers? Were there other options open to him? These and other questions ought to be raised as we reflect upon the intricacies of his decision-making process, and the consequences for our lives today under the changing wisdom of leaders who need also to be aware of the dynamics of change, willing always to learn for the sake of humankind, knowing that we are all connected in the *imago Dei*, to be faithful stewards of our Creator-God working together as a team of soul-mates that is greater any one nation alone can accomplish.

Scripture to consider:
Genesis 1:24-31; 2:1-25
Psalm 73 (doing God's Will in heaven and on earth)
I Kings 3:1-28
Isaiah 2:1-4
Micah 4:1-4
Matthew Chapters 7, 17 & 18
James: Chapters 4 & 5 and also, I John 4:16-21

Articles and a film for classroom and neighborhood discussion:
Time Magazine on August 28, 2017 dedicated several major articles as a **Special Report on the theme--*Hate In America*** with a team of writers on the Post-Civil War tragedy in Charlottesville, Virginia (8/12/17): Nancy Gibbs, *Will The Nation Succeed Where The President Failed?;* Michael Scherer and Alex Altman, *Bigots, Boosted By The Bully Pulpit*; Jon Meacham, *America Hate, A History;* Eddie S. Glaude Jr., *What White America Must Do Next*; Ilhan Omar, *Unity Will Take Generations;* Tavis Smiley, *From Selma To Charlottesville, The Ghosts Of Our Past* and John Grisham, *A Town Violated.*

Foreign Affairs: Who Will Run the World? America, China, and Global Order, Jan./Feb. Vol.98 No.1, 2019.

Roderick M. Kramer**, "*Rethinking Trust*", *Harvard Business Review,* June 9, 2009, pp.69-77. In this connection read John Grisham's recent book, T*he Rooster Bar,* Doubleday, and look up Paul Campos' factual article in *Atlantic*, September 2014 which sparked the writing of Grisham's *Rooster Bar* novel

Shane Claiborne & Michael Martin, *"Guns into Garden Tools", The Christian Century, March 13, 2019, and for further information contact RAWtools, Inc.* learning how to melt down weapons into garden tools around the world. *The Christian Century,* March 13, 2019.

Green Book, a recent Oscar winning film is based on a true story of Don Shirley a professionally recognized jazz pianist of Jamaican-American heritage and Shirley's driver Tony Vallelonga with his *Green Book.*

Chapter 8. Common Passwords for God & Neighbors

"No one seems to like me," said a girl to me one day. "Do you like yourself? I asked. She replied in a hesitant tone. "I don't know. I seem to have so many doubts about my self-worth, and I think even less of my classmates who ignore me. I interrupted her: "Hey, wait a minute! God cares for you, and also for your classmates as well". God's caring can be universal and more inclusive than ours, which we tend to overlook when hit by storms. We need to remind ourselves as caring stewards of God's creation that we are responsible for the environment and its surrounding life for God loves the world, not just us. (John 3:16) Jesus taught this message throughout his earthly ministry.

Yet, I knew that this teenager like many others was preoccupied with her own concerns, seeking affirmation of her own self-worth with her peers and with God. She was burdened with negative feelings and observations. Underlying her uncertainty lay a sense of alienation based on broken relationships. She felt rejected. I searched for an appropriate biblical passage to boost her feelings and concerns. I had a biblical passage in mind, but it didn't seem to fit the moment. Have you had a similar experience in conversations and decided to refrain from offering further remarks? We agreed to get together again soon.

Recalling my experience without revealing her name, I mentioned the gist of the conversation with two colleagues over coffee. One biblical scholar responded by saying, "Is there really anything on 'self-acceptance' in our Bibles? Scripture calls us 'sinners' with a lifestyle that might be questionable at times". His tone seemed too judgmental to me. My concern was to give her hope. Any further discussion with colleagues on sin would need to wait for another occasion.

For now, I wanted that teenager to be aware that judgment on ourselves belongs to God, and ought to be reserved for greater discernment by someone trained in these matters who can show wisdom. When we met a second time, she and I engaged in searching for ways to find greater meaning and purpose in our lives, taking into account that we are embedded in God's image, the *imago Dei*. As our discussion ended, she led in pray to give thanks for her life. She thanked God for strengthening and enabling us to fulfill God's Will daily, adding meaning to our lives, teaching us how to act with goodwill towards others.

A few weeks later at another coffee break with faculty colleagues, one of them referred to the previous discussion asking if Scripture addressed *self-acceptance*. "I have been thinking about it for some time", said my colleague. "As you know I teach psychology not Bible, but nevertheless I thought it odd to think there is no scriptural reference to *self-acceptance* as one of our biblical scholars mentioned since we are sinners". The psychology professor went on to say, "There may be no specific scriptural passage on self-acceptance, but we are instructed, nevertheless, in our sacred text, *'to love our neighbors as ourselves'"*.

Implicit in this injunction, the psychologist indicated, is the need to accept ourselves at a deeper level. We can't love our neighbors without first loving and accepting ourselves. His Bible colleague responded excitedly, "That's just it! We are unable to love our neighbors because we actually have trouble loving ourselves! We haven't come to terms yet with the nature of our sinfulness". We knew then that our discussion was not over, the coffee break however was. I suspect at the heart of this discussion on self-acceptance and human sinfulness is whether or not we are willing to believe that in creation we were all spiritually embedded with the *imago Dei*. If so, did our Creator-God design humankind to be divided or united racially or otherwise, given the realities of global diversity with its many histories of spiritual and religious differences over the centuries? Over the centuries there have been many ecumenical and interfaith discussions, but thus far no grand resolve of these differences in accepting the spirit of the *imago Dei* as a reality. Accepting diversity has brought us closer to God's Will overcoming wrongful interpretations of the past but has not yet brought sufficient peace to end battles from past histories thereby weakening any religious voice on the international stage to keep *human life human in all aspects of collective lives.*

From a biblical perspective, esteem and acceptance require healthy relationships and a spirit of thanksgiving in praise to our Creator-God whose care is present in spite of the rough edges and complex cultures of faith. An international password in everyone's language would be helpful in an interconnected world. There is a short list of words that can be our passwords globally.

We can begin meaningfully with the words, *"Thank You"* spoken in every tongue. Another word not often heard is, "forgiveness". Asking for forgiveness or even practicing it in relationships is not a sign of weakness, but rather a sign of inner strength. To restore *forgiveness* as a *password* would heal broken relationships. Forgiveness gains traction when the healing process backed with humility soothes scars. Neither side can forget suffering. Forgiveness does not imply that we can overlook what has happened. Forgiveness is the process of learning to forgo resentment even while remembering. The cross of Jesus continues to be a difficult symbol for onlookers--

believers as well as nonbelievers—inviting all to practice forgiving love in the face of broken relationships. Are we willing to accept the challenge?

Offering thanks to God can be a slow learning process with many social infections leaving us in a lockdown status unable to launch a pathway to a fuller life, afraid of the next pandemic on the horizon, a barrier to rebuilding a vibrant community in the midst of pain and losses of yesterday. Recovering our capacity to give thanks for God's mercy is the password to renewal. Gratitude can free us from self-imposed enslavement and restore spiritual health energizing us in a changing world. Thankfulness and forgiveness are keys to open ourselves and our communities to tomorrow's society with displaced friends and migrants eager to work with their talents to rebuild towns and cities for a fuller life in a world that is finally awakening to its true interconnectedness based on everyone's divine worth whatever our cultural backgrounds. Our roots are in the common ground of creation, the *imago Dei*. This has been told long ago in the stories of our sacred text—the *Hebrew Bible (Old Testament) beginning with the Book of Genesis: 1: 26-2:4*. The message of *Jesus's ministry (New Testament Bible)* is a continuation of the essential story that God has not forsaken us in spite of our shortcomings, urging us now to rejoice in the spirit of the *imago Dei*, teaching us to accept humankind in its diversity as soulmates praising our Creator-God for our journey in life.

It shouldn't surprise us to see how Jesus responded to the young lawyer's anxiety to guarantee eternal life. He invited the lawyer to consider giving up his possessions and to join him in his journey of faith. Was this invitation too costly for the lawyer to accept as he considered Jesus' appearance and lack of belongings? (Luke18:18-30) In our changing world today, I wonder if believers and non-believers realize how much they have at stake in approaching tomorrow's crossroads as they travel nationally and globally? Is there a spiritual compass for all? Is life the same on either side of the walls and fences we construct as our borders? I suspect these and other questions will be discussed in neighborhoods and classrooms as we design our individual biblical passports with candor.

In connection with our biblical passports, another aspect for discussion is the use of mottos and pledges as passwords heard in public gatherings, assemblies and classrooms to lift spirits and address anxieties, such as *"In God We Trust", "God bless America" and the Pledge of Allegiance to our nation's flag.* These expressions may offer more comfort to citizens than non-citizens in uniting a nation of believers. How do non-believers who are also citizens feel? And what would we do with our nation's*, **Great Seal as One Nation which presently reads—E pluribus unum (out of many, one)** adopted by an Act of Congress in 1782? Do we wish to update this seal in our changing world, as we move on to tomorrow's spatial age? Perhaps the Psalmist of old was wiser than us when he declared to humankind: *"Know that the Lord is God. It is he that made us, and we are his; we are his people, and the sheep of his pasture. Enter his gates with thanksgiving, and his courts with praise. Give thanks to him, bless his holy name." (Psalm. 100:3-4)*

Scripture to consider:
Genesis, James, and Philippians read in their entirety would be beneficial.
Psalms 23, 90, 100, 138 & 139
Matthew 18:1-7 & 19:13-15
Luke 18: 18-30; 35-43
Galatians 6: 1-10

Films for group discussion:
The Shack film focuses on when we find ourselves blaming God for the tragic events in our lives.

Invictus focuses on the faith and struggles of Nelson Mandela and his colleagues in South Africa.

Another movie of note, *The Promise* retells historic events based on the major *1915 Armenian Genocide* in which Turkey perpetrated and still officially denies the loss of more than a million and a half Armenians plus the displacement of other minorities including Greeks, many of whom were able to escape to Greece and neighboring countries. *The Promise* is based on Franz Werfel's book, *The Forty Days of Musa Dagh.*

Part III: Be Generous

Chapter 9. Ethics of Generosity from the Epistle of James

Some years ago, Doris and I enjoyed a cruise along Alaska's inland coastal line. I was invited to be one of the ship's chaplains for the cruise. To our pleasant surprise, two very special guests on board were Mr. and Mrs. James A. Michener. Holland America was celebrating the publication of his latest book, *Alaska*, which made the best-seller's list at the time.

Raised a Quaker, Mr. Michener also attended Presbyterian churches with his wife; our conversations revealed several mutual friends. During the cruise, Mr. Michener shared his outlook on life, as well as his pattern for writing books. At one point, he remarked that he saw himself as a "Jamesian Christian."

Let's take a closer look at a verse in James which expresses Michener's faith. "Real religion in the sight of God is this: *'To go to the help of orphans and widows in their distress and keep oneself unstained by the world.'"* (James 1:2) Michener explained his

115

preferred understanding of Christianity pointed to demonstrable deeds rather than words or logic. "You see," he said, "I was a foundling child, raised by a Quaker woman whose demonstrated love was my basic introduction to the Christian faith."

"But do you know", I remarked, "that the Epistle of James has been controversial in the history of the church's canon? It did not receive easy acceptance into the New Testament." Martin Luther objected to it as a "straw epistle" believing it was James' interpretation of the Christian faith which conflicted with the Apostle Paul's emphasis on *justification by faith through grace* as expressed in Paul's Epistle to the Romans. (Romans 4: 13-5: 21)

Michener's Jamesian interpretation is based on the caring example of Jesus during his earthly ministry who demonstrated that faith and action belong together. The Epistle of James emphasizes that the depth of faith is evidenced by deeds which reveal the nature of our faith. This was the theme behind the life of James, calling us to be *"doers of the word, and not hearers only, deceiving yourselves."* (James 1:22)

What implication does *Jamesian Christianity* have for believers today in the marketplace, at worship, and in our private study as we seek to apply the sacred texts to our everyday lives? Can the Epistle of James serve as an *ethical guidebook* for a diverse cross-section of humanity seeking direction as global caregivers in a

116

changing world? We are all in the process of seeking common ground to execute shared priorities that will benefit humankind. *In short, can we do good together locally and globally as goodwill ambassadors as we build beneficial trust with one another?* Is this also the underlying theme of CBS's long-standing television program—*Madame Secretary-- with its interfaith aspects for problem-solving and trust-building among nations facing mutual crossroads of conflict?*

From a cursory investigation, I have discovered that the Epistle of James is largely a forgotten text among many believers. Sunday school classes and pulpits generally place more attention on the Pauline Epistles than the Epistle of James. Perhaps Martin Luther was right in referring to James as a "straw epistle". And yet, I find this slim Epistle with only five chapters to be a useful manual of wisdom for the renewal of ethics personally and collectively within all aspects of our global society today. Not long ago, a former colleague at Pittsburgh Seminary, Professor Dale C. Allison, Jr. completed and published an extensive major commentary on the Epistle of James. Professor Allison is now serving on the faculty of Princeton Theological Seminary and has enriched students at both institutions and far beyond to appreciate the value of the Epistle of James in emphasizing the ***ethics of generosity.*** Would this approach seem unrealistic in today's global society?

What primary focus can we hope for as we prepare seminarians and laity in many professional fields to be more ethically alert in their areas of research and service to society? Listen to some limited responses I have received. One alumna mentioned that the focus of graduate education ought to be centered on one all-important question: "Who is Jesus for us today whatever our profession might be?" An issue of *Time Magazine* raised a similar question some time ago as it discussed the controversial film *The Last Temptation of Christ,* based on Nikos Kazantzakis' novel. *The* cover-page for that issue was a composite of 17 images of Jesus dating from the Sixth Century to the present, illustrating the hermeneutical complexity of this challenging question— *"Who was Jesus?"* Another graduate responded on the need for an interfaith emphasis after reading *The New York Times* columnist, Nicholas Kristof's provocative article, *"What religion would Jesus belong to in our present changing ethos"?* Should Christians or Muslims be engaged in converting one another, or for that matter, is any person of faith or no faith really able to listen to another truthfully? Are interfaith spiritual leaders and their followers willing to commit their limited financial resources, time, and talent to promote international encounters to establish a common understanding for peace and justice? Are we willing to educate potential goodwill ambassadors to help societies across international borders to tackle complex issues facing humanity in this inter-disciplinary age? Can graduate professional schools like medicine, law, religious schools, social work centers, nursing, etc. educate new leaders in a multicultural and interdisciplinary fashion to address our growing

118

curiosity with renewed efforts to survive in spite of yesterday's social and religious barriers facing us? Humankind, I believe, has the emerging urge to restore God's Will in place of ours--uncovering the spirit of the *imago Dei* within us to care for one another without any self-centered borders, fulfilling our essential stewardship before the just God of our universe.

The **"Eighth Day"** mentioned in our Bibles, highlights that God's calendar extends beyond our human measurements of time. God has been waiting for our generosity; we have as yet not reached the hopes of many, the divine promise holds countless blessings for us to distribute in God's name. The spiritual fact is that God's grace continues to shower us with nature's resources, while relying on our stewardship to distribute faithfully, justly and generously to the needs of humankind and all created life around us. We are shamefully aware that our past stewardship has been less than generous, and we are grateful that our Creator-God hasn't given-up on us yet. (Psalm 138) Human failings were well understood by Jesus during his ministry on earth, as he wisely taught his followers to pray with gratitude asking that, *"God's Will, not theirs, be done on earth as well as in heaven."*

Scripture to consider:

Psalms 74 to 77 & 85 (our ways vs. God's pathway)
Proverbs 3 (Above all trust in God for guidance.)
Matthew 6: 9-13 (Jesus teaching his followers to pray.)

Colossians 2:20-23, 3:14-17
I Thessalonians chapters 1 and 2 (on generosity witnessed in its varied forms.)
James 1: 22-27
Professor Dale Allison's extensive commentary on the *Epistle of James* can enrich group discussions. His study is,*"A Critical and Exegetical Commentary on the Epistle of James"*, Bloomsbury T&T Clark, 2013, U.K.

Books and articles for classroom and neighborhood discussion:

For a wider understanding on the *ethics of generosity*, see the discussion on *"The 'Golden Rule' among the World Religions"* published in a booklet by the Weisfeld Foundation through the generosity of Gerald and Vera Weisfeld of Scotland with The Global Ethic Foundation by Count K.K. von der Groeben in Tubingen, Germany. The complete title of the booklet is *"World Religions, Universal Peace, Global Ethics"*, with an introduction by Professor Hans Kung. For Kung's interfaith insights, see his book, *Tracing the Way: Spiritual Dimensions of the World Religions,* Continuum, U.K.

Christopher De Bellaigue, *The Islamic Enlightment; The Struggle Between Faith And Reason, 1798 To Modern Times*, Live Right Publishing Corporation, NY

Emily J. Levine and Mitchell L. Stevens, "The Right Way to Fix Universities", *The New York Times*,

December 1, 2017. Levine at the University of North Carolina and Stevens at Stanford University offer together insights on the ethics of generosity.

David Bentley Hart, *Are Christians Supposed to be Communists? The New York Times,* November 11, 2017; and *Why Do People Believe in Hell? NYT,* 1/11/2020. Dr. Hart is a fellow at the Notre Dame Institute for Advanced Study.

Nicholas Kristof, *"Our Chess Champ Has A Home", The New York Times,* March 24, 2019. Kristof highlights a wonderful example of seeing the ethics of generosity centered on a young eight year old Nigerian boy, Tanitoluwa Adewumi who lived with his refugee family legally at a Manhattan shelter and was soon enrolled in the public school system where he learned the game of chess, winning *the New York State Chess Championship* for his age category, which in turn inspired his parents to look after the needs of others at the shelter as well as their love-ones and many others remaining in Nigeria.

Nick Hanauer, *"Education Isn't Enough", The Atlantic,* July 2019. The author is a successful entrepreneur and venture capitalist who confesses that like many rich Americans, he gave millions to improve schools in order to heal the country's ills but has discovered he was wrong. He now believes that fighting inequality must come first. This can be a lively topic for a group discussion.

Chapter 10. What Money Can't Buy!

Holidays and birthdays can be times of expectation and disappointment. Many disappointments are due to limited bank accounts or zero savings. The familiar story of Dickens' ***Christmas Carol*** with Tiny Tim, Bob Cratchit and Mr. Scrooge is not simply a story about the scarcity of funds, but also about the discovery that gracious giving is at the heart of relationships within our diverse and needy societies.

The aim in this chapter is not to debate whether or not money is important; most of us have probably experienced, even painfully perhaps, the necessity of money. We see plenty of evidence of what money can do to enhance our situation and improve institutions as well. Certainly, resources are necessary to enhance facilities and program developments within cities, towns and neighborhoods. We know that adequate income makes it possible to enjoy comfortable homes, as well as recreational and educational perks. Is money then, the key to happiness and our sense of security? There's no doubt that good paying jobs are really necessary in communities and wages can't remain static.

Listeners and readers of daily news may recall the headlines informing us that Doris Duke, the tobacco heiress had died at age 80. *The New York Times* headline read: *"Doris Duke, 80, Heiress of Great Wealth Whose Money Couldn't Buy Happiness."* She left behind three homes in New Jersey, Rhode Island and Hawaii, with an estate of nearly two billion dollars. Divorced twice, she was single most of her life and in search of authentic relationships. Her father died when she was 12; a premature daughter died in a Honolulu hospital after only 24 hours of life; and her best friend was killed when Ms. Duke in her car accidentally hit him with her car. Hers was a life of tragedies; Doris Duke tried to make peace with life through her charities and travels. She remarked to a friend when she was 33 years old that her vast fortune was often a barrier to happiness. Ms. Duke said, "All that money is a problem sometimes…. every time after I have gone out with a man a few times, he starts to tell me how much he loves me. *But how can I know if he really means it? How can I ever be sure?"* Her unhappiness was keenly felt throughout her lifetime.

Most of us are not in her circle of wealth. Most of us, I suspect wouldn't say no if a few million dollars were bequeathed to us. Wouldn't the income from those millions help ease present worries and increase a measure of happiness in our lives? Doesn't money buy peace of mind? And couldn't we all use some extra cash? On a trip to Washington, D.C., I was appalled at the number of homeless and hungry persons seen on the streets of our nation's capital. I couldn't help but think that some money would indeed offer these folks stability and a measure of happiness. Survival means food and safety for rich and poor alike; however, there is a price to pay that we have long since discovered. There is no free lunch! The wages of success have been earned unless there's a pandemic requiring added funds or an unexpected inheritance to calm us.

Those who have experienced poverty as well as wealth will tell you with candor. *"We have been rich, and we have been poor, but rich is better."* Wouldn't you agree? Are you willing then to buy the proposition that money buys happiness? But what is happiness, anyway? *What is it that money can't buy?* This is a significant question as we think of practicing goodwill. In an attempt to answer these questions, I have conducted my own "Calian Poll." I quickly discovered there are many definitions of happiness; each reflects the context in which persons find themselves. For instance, at a coffee break discussion with faculty and students at Pittsburgh Seminary where I taught, I learned that happiness for seminarians is receiving a call from a congregation, recovering a treasured object believed to be lost, being comfortable with one's self, and enjoying a measure of self-confidence.

For faculty colleagues, happiness is having a book or article accepted for publication, delivering a stimulating lecture, hearing students buzz the hallways in excitement over the exchange of ideas that took place in class. Happiness can also be found in those moments when we have the courage to stand-up for what we believe matters, to take a position on an issue and to defend it well.

Returning home that evening from the office, I reflected on happiness for myself: Happiness is taking a walk with my wife, cuddling grandchildren, having family and friends gather for celebrations; happiness is also good health, exquisite music, former students and family members doing well vocationally, being with old friends and discovering new ones. *In the final analysis, can any of these experiences be bought?*

Happiness no doubt for many of us is having a job that provides not only an income, but purpose and fulfillment to our lives. I was often asked, "Were you happy being president of the seminary? My usual reply was, "80% of the time". A recent book by Jonathan Rauch, *The Happiness Curve* (Thomas Dune) alerts us to be more aware of how aging changes our outlook and widens our acceptance and understanding of happiness. We aren't expected to walk around looking for a Hollywood version of fulfillment as we confront unexpected realities and setbacks. Our lives are engaged in a convergence of many worlds that contribute to the complexity and confusion of our times.

We need to ask, which world do we live in, before deciding not only money matters, but also the direction and goals we wish to pursue. What is in our best interest as individuals and as a community? What can money buy or not buy whether in a trade war, religious war, gun war, drug war or some other war. Do we really know what is truly healthy for humankind and can it be bought? How do we proceed to design a meaningful biblical passport in keeping with our favorite sacred texts as we seek to build bridges of understanding instead of remaining in ours or someone's Tower of Babel?

Many, I suspect, would like to exchange some frustrations and disappointments at work for a more ideal situation. The real world is never without blemishes. There is no "perfect world". Whatever your image of happiness might be, it needs to be related to reality and be affordable. Such is often not the case. For many, happiness is tied to wishes, desires and dreams. As a consequence, many of us are always searching for ideal employment, that big deal, the perfect marriage, the perfect church, temple or mosque, the flawless child, total personality harmony, and recognition or fame that never seems to happen or is simply taking too long. Fred Rogers of *Mr. Rogers' Neighborhood* fame could tell you many stories as he brought cheer to the lives of young people and their parents during his lifetime career *as an ambassador* of goodwill on television and in person as well. Ordained as a

Presbyterian minister following his graduation from Pittsburgh Seminary, his was a unique ministry on the television screen. Fred spoke to our graduates and their families and friends at the Seminary's 200th anniversary commencement service in 1994. He shared the biblical vision behind his life of service to others, with gratitude to God for enabling him and his creative television team including his wife Joanne to fulfill their outreach of loving care to their neighborhood that stretches around the world. He placed emphasis on every child and every adult to offer their unique gifts in service to others in the spirit of the *imago Dei*. Unfortunately, many of us fall short of that goal, seeking a shortcut to happiness through the lottery system. We live under the illusion that happiness comes with the big win. Is having more money really a panacea for happiness? No doubt it would help many persons and institutions facing budget crunches. Recently, I heard a church treasurer say to the congregation, "Happiness is having a positive cash flow after the pandemic." Our religious structures and professional schools where I have taught, are no exception, constantly in need of financial support to educate their students for effective service to humankind wherever they serve.

In all situations, we need to place the financial needs of organizations and individuals in perspective to the level of happiness desired in reaching goals. There is no doubt that there is some correlation between personal income and personal well-being. For the poor, money is often required to buy a measure of happiness and health such as the basic necessities of food, shelter and safety. However, economists and policymakers have also noted that the desire for more money does not taper off as personal income increases. Many are unwilling to recognize this. Our consuming psyche drives us on and on; we never seem to have enough money to buy all that we desire. We find ourselves acquiring more and more in response to our insatiable appetites. Our homes, basements and garages fill up. Perhaps we ought to appreciate this; how else would we supply merchandise for the annual church bazaars? Having less might actually make our efforts at downsizing easier as well as simplifying our lifestyle.

By the age of 15, it is said that the average American teen has witnessed more than 330,000 commercials on TV. We have been dehumanized into buyers; the labels "consumer" and "Patriotic American" seem inseparable. What has happened to the biblical ethic for thrift and simplicity? How are we addressing our longing for spiritual growth and enduring values? How can we enhance the quality of our lives to provide a more satisfying life beyond waste-management of discarded items? In short, what is the ethics of enduring values, of success itself? Have we the right to claim greatness on any scale in light of our practices and lifestyle? Whatever has happened to the authentic spirit of generosity, as we purchase more and more from our stores and also online with its timely convenience?

Spiritual maturity recognizes that happiness depends on relationships, not the build-up of monetary assets. In fact, with more money, we begin to think and feel like Doris Duke, wondering about the real motives of those who befriend us. Is this why we relate so positively to the Cinderella story? Do we identify with the prince who in his search for true beauty found it in genuine authentic relationships? No one is satisfied with superficial relationships found at many social gatherings. What is fulfilling are authentic relationships spiritual and human. This is what Fred Rogers' neighborhood is all about. These relationships are keys that release happiness in our lives. We can't buy honest relationships. Doris Duke was right about that. Wholesome relationships grow out of bonding that involves joy and tears, strength and vulnerability.

The test of friendship is found when we truly wish our friend well. How many persons in life are there, that truly wish us well? Unfortunately, our society divides us into competitors. Sometimes we collect IOUs, seeking leverage over one another; we also seek vengeance to "even the score." To a large extent, we live in an unhappy society absorbing 6 o'clock news with its political complaints and neighborhood fights. We always welcome the spirit of generosity at special seasons of the year that offers relief from the competitive jungle in which we find ourselves most of the year.

The Psalms from our Bibles also offer us a clue to happiness. Far more than the monetary build-up of assets, happiness lies in exercising our faith, our trust that the Will of God is in our best interest. To believe otherwise is to invite despair and disappointment. Note how the Psalmist writes: (from Psalm 40: 4-8)

Happy are those who make the Lord their trust,
Who do not turn to the proud, to those who go astray
after false gods.
You have multiplied, O Lord my God, your wondrous
deeds and your
thoughts toward us; none can compare with you. Were I
to proclaim and tell of them, they would be more than
can be counted.
Sacrifice and offering you do not desire, but you have
given me an open
ear. Burnt offering and sin offering you have not
required.
Then I said, Here I am: in the scroll of the book it is
written of me.
I delight to do your will. O my God; your law is within
my heart

To pursue the will of God is the believer's path to happiness. Our journey into eternity begins on earth expressing God's ethics of generosity. On this highway of life, God wishes us well in spite of all the zigs and zags ahead. God wishes not only to be family to us, but for us to follow the divine pathway Jesus taught, witnessed in the action of the "good Samaritan"

131

forecasting God's generosity, and reminding us that we are all created in the *imago Dei (God's image)*. Our Creator deserves our complete trust, as the Psalmist declares, as we experience divine grace in our lives.

Happiness is found then, in our willingness to journey with God from sunrise to sunrise without reservation, to cultivate this divine/human relationship whatever our conditions in life might be. ***Trust in God is the foundation for happiness.*** It can't be purchased; you need to prayerfully pursue it in faith, knowing that God's Will has its own sign-posts to direct us, expressed through our sacred texts: *"All things work together for good, for those called according to God's purpose."* (Romans 8:28)

Life has meaning when there is purpose, a sense of call that fills lives with direction, *completing* God's agenda, not ours, for the world God loves. Pursuing God's Will gives our journey divine depth. Biblical passports can guide our steps, inspire us to reflect on the *imago Dei* as we meet strangers, and to acknowledge that we need to labor together to bring peace and justice. This requires a *"soul to soul"* attitude within us to overcome the negative spirit of conflict that makes it so difficult to resolve our differences in the competitive marketplace where distrust dominates and God's image as soul-mates is lost, and along with it *God's Golden Rule* inspired at the beginning of creation.

From a sacred and secular perspective money is necessary, but it doesn't promise enduring trust in families, among colleagues, trading partners or among rivals. Self-interest rather than the Golden Rule has been the basic metric in monetary relations among individuals, tribes, and nations. We have a long way to travel in building deeper trust beyond what money in all its varied forms can buy, wherever we travel in our Creator's universe. The divine wisdom for financial governance continues to escape us along with mutual humility.

Scripture to consider:
Psalms 40:1-10; 146 to 150
Proverbs 4
Luke 10:29-37; 18:18-30
Romans 8:28
Luke 10:29-37; 18:18-30

Books and articles for classroom and neighborhood discussions:
Brad Stone, *The Everything Store: Jeff Bezos And the Age of Amazon*, Little, Brown & Company, New York; and Jeffrey D. Sachs, *COMMONWEALTH: Economics for A Crowded Planet*, The Penguin Press, New York; and John Hunter, *World Peace and Other 4th-Grade Achievements*, Houghton Mifflin Harcourt, Boston

Tracy Kidder, *Mountains Beyond Mountains*, Random House, New York & *A Truck Full of Money*, Random House, New York

Ronald A Heifetz, *Leadership Without Easy Answers*, Harvard University Press, Cambridge, Massachusetts

Michael J. Sandel, *What Money Can't Buy: The Moral Limits of Markets,* Farrar Straus And Giroux, New York

William C. Remple, *"The Gambler: How Penniless Dropout Kirk Kerkorian Became the Greatest Deal Maker in Capitalist History",* Dey Street (William Morrow) The author is a noted journalist who followed Kerkorian's modest beginnings, born to poor Armenian immigrant parents in Fresno, California. Kirk's early life gave him his first lessons in the *"College of Hard Knocks",* dropping out of school at the eighth grade to assist his parents with family needs during the depression. Kerkorian's *life in many respects is an important lesson in what money can buy and also what it can't buy.* This quiet but ambitious young man never forgot his friends in need nor his Armenian heritage. He is regarded as a major donor in rebuilding today's modern Armenian Republic after its major earthquake of 1988.

Paul Sullivan, *"Inside the Wealth Divide: Not only has the gulf grown between the haves and the have-nots, but so has the gap between haves and the have-mores"*, a special *Wealth Section of The New York Times,* Nov. 12, 2017.

Tali Sharot, *"The Science of Optimism: Hope isn't rational—so why are* humans wired for it?", *Time Magazine,* June 6, 2011

David Brooks, *"Giving Away Your Billion", The New York Times,* June 20/2017

Kathryn Tanner, *"What Does Grace Have to Do with Money?", Harvard Divinity Bulletin,* Spring,2002

Cornel West and Robert P. George, *"Dr. King's Radical Biblical Vision", The Wall Street Journal,* April 6, 2018.

Marc Gunther, *"God and Business: The Surprising Quest for Spiritual Renewal In the American Workplace", Fortune,* July 9, 2001

Chapter 11. When Is a Friend, a _Friend?_

When are friends authentic? How many friends do we really have? Many of us have observed through disappointing experiences, *that there are fair weather friends and then there are true friends.*

Some use the term "friend" rather loosely; we tend to confuse friendship with acquaintanceship. Many strangers and immigrants to our shores have commented that we Americans have an underdeveloped understanding of friendship. We too quickly call someone a friend; for a non-American this is amusing. I suspect we would all admit that authentic friendship normally requires time; we process a relationship through a period of mutual self-discovery. Americans, however, seem to expect instant friendships. We tend to call most persons we meet friends after an initial meeting or conversation, but upon further reflection we find this is not true.

When then is a friend, **a Friend?** Could we say that the story of our lives can be traced through the tale of friendships made and broken? Who is and who isn't our friend becomes evident over time by actions and behavior? We must never lose sight of the fact that friendships are also fragile. How can we distinguish genuine friends among our countless relationships? The biblical passage of John 15:12-17 offers us three situations to test the nature of true friendship.

In speaking to his disciples, Jesus uses the word "friends" three times in John 15. The first use in verse 13 highlights the ultimate test of friendship indicating that, "Greater love has no one than this, that someone lays down one's life for their friends." I suspect we wonder at times, if anyone we know is willing to be measured by that criterion.

Nevertheless, there are those who can testify to the loving quality of sacrifice witnessed in a parent's love for their children, grandparent's devotion to grandchildren, or a sibling's act of love. We have seen such acts of sacrificial friendship in times of crisis – floods, earthquakes and in personal times of deep grief. Such sacrificial friendship and kindness are experienced in the donation of a transplanted organ that gives life and hope; the organ donor becomes an unexpected friend whose generosity sustains us.

Others have experienced sacrificial acts of friendship in times of war. In the film *Saving Private Ryan,* the opening scene an elderly man (Ryan) visits with great emotion the graveside of the captain who gave his life in battle so that Private Ryan might live. The foremost level of friendship involves sacrificial love. It points to deeds rather than speeches and promises. The story of the Good Samaritan is the story of true friendship exercised unexpectedly and graciously by a traveling stranger who is actually a friend in disguise sent from God.

Perhaps the actor Jimmy Stewart summed it up best in his book, It's *A Wonderful Life* when he said, "Remember, no one is a failure who has friends." Friends are those willing to express their relationship in loving deeds and not simply in words. The crucifixion of Jesus on the cross highlights the reality that genuine human interaction involves sacrifice. To the extent that we are willing to trade our life for a friend is the ultimate test of friendship. From this standpoint, how many friends do we really have?

The second criterion for friendship according to Jesus requires respect and a willingness to follow our friends' wishes. "You are my friends," says Jesus in verse 14, "if you do what I command." *Implicit in friendship is followership that includes the willingness to listen.* This is not always easy to accomplish as the disciples discovered. Building friendships according to Jesus is a matter of caring and critical listening. Jesus was indicating to his follower's past and present that the command to listen is an imperative, if we are to have enduring relationships that enable genuine friendship to flourish.

In our fast-paced lives, we take too little time to listen to one another. How then do we have time to become a community of genuine friends? We seem to have our "answers" before we have heard the question. We rush in to offer solutions to a friend, when what is truly needed first is a listening ear. Is this why talk shows on radio and television have expanded in recent years? Does it reflect the public's need to have someone on the air listening to us? Is it our desire to have someone of importance befriend us, as seen on CBS's recent Sunday evening program, "God Friended Me"?

In today's professionalized society, we have paid "friends" to listen to our concerns. Friendship essentially operates on practicing acceptance, not attempting to change or "improve" the other person as our first order of business. Friendship provides the freedom to disagree without exerting pressures on others to conform. Ours is indeed a lonely world in search of listeners. Who will take time to hear us in a caring way without looking at their watches or listening to something else on their head piece?

The third insight for friendship from Jesus encourages us to share ourselves, overcoming the tendency to hide behind our weaknesses and faults. It takes courage to share our vulnerability, to let our secrets and failed ambitions be known. Jesus said to his disciples in verse 15, "I no longer call you servants, because a servant does not know his master's business. Instead, I have called you friends, for everything I have learned from

my heavenly Father I have made known to you."
Sharing one's self places trust in another, creating a
relationship that leads to friendship.

Some years ago, in a workshop with business and
professional leaders in which I participated, the speaker
asked those of us present, to write down our goals and
ambitions for the next five years. Since the workshop
had already been meeting for several days, he suggested
that the participants turn to someone they might
consider as a friend and share their hopes for the future.
One workshop member was overheard whispering,
"Hell, I don't have any friends, that's why I'm
successful." In the atmosphere of such a society only
counterfeit relationships will emerge. Genuine
friendships become a real luxury that no one can afford.
Have we already become such a society in which
authentic friendships are unaffordable? Have we lost the
meaning of friendship?

Perhaps the true status of bankruptcy is discovering that
we haven't any friends, that no one really cares for us
regardless of our financial worth. I have heard that more
than once; it no longer surprises me. Is lasting
friendship incompatible with achieving success in
today's market-driven society?

It is currently said, that we have become a culture of
distrust. In practice we tend to share, if at all, in a very
selective or secretive manner. We never seem to tell any
single friend everything, but only small bits and pieces

of ourselves. This often makes us appear inconsistent and contradictory. Apparently, we are willing to pay this price in a distrusting society. Basic mistrust is endemic to the building up of lasting and deepening relationships where we can really become friends to one another. To say that we are a society in search of listeners, is to admit that we have become a society lacking trusting relationships. Fulfillment is not found simply in chasing dollars or seeking status, but in building healthy and trusting relationships that can become genuine friendships. Perhaps we have created today an invisible poverty, no time for authentic friendships. The absence of human friendships makes a difference in the quality of our lives. Our depression and loneliness are to a large extent our own fault, as we reflect on our style of living whatever the size of our community might be.

Finally, let's be willing to admit that there are no perfect friendships, just as we have discovered that there are no perfect relatives. Some might feel otherwise, blessed with unique family members who appear to be "perfect". Whatever the case, friends of our youth and strangers we have met later in life have now also become friends, but generally tend to refrain from telling the whole story of their lives. We seem to live within a constant process of discovery, revising our earlier judgments of one another with added experiences as told on the Ted talk-shows. As we design our individual biblical passports, we will be further enlightened by one another's experiences, slowly realizing that we are all truly embedded in the spirit of the *imago Dei* as we truly wish one another well. We are all actually anointed with names, each called to be special stewards of our Creator-God wherever life's journey leads us to fulfill God's Will.

Scripture to consider:

Psalms Chapters 81-85 (the Israelites wavered in their friendships with God too.)
John 15:12-17
Galatians 5:1-6
I John 4 "My dear friends, don't believe everything you hear..."
Revelation 22:1-5; 12-21

Books and articles for classroom and neighborhood groups:

Robert D. Putnam & David E. Campbell, *AMERICAN GRACE: How Religion Divides and Unites Us,* Simon & Schuster, New York

Marc Freedman, *ENCORE: Finding Work That Matters in the Second Half of Life,* Public Affairs, New York. This is a helpful volume for an aging community that refuses to retire, volunteering their skills and knowledge to assist others in need.

N.J. Enfield, *How We Talk: The Inner Workings Of Conversations*, Basic Books, New York. Enfield is

Professor of Linguistics at the University of Sydney, Australia. His research uncovers meaning and closeness in the minutiae of chatter.

Christopher Mele, "Some COFFEE Shops Are Skipping Wi-Fi to Encourage Customers to Actually Talk", The New York Times, May 10, 2017

Kevin Kirkland, "The Art of Friendship", The Pittsburgh Post-Gazette, 9/ 21/13

Film discussion on Fred Rogers, *"Won't You Be My Neighbor?"* Roger's life and TV programs illustrate his deep understanding of friendship that embodies the spirit of the *imago Dei*. Doris and I regard Fred and his wife Joanne as examples of *goodwill ambassadors* during our years living in Pittsburgh, grateful that they included the Pittsburgh Seminary community as part of their neighborhood.

Part IV: Practice Moderation

Chapter 12. What's at the Heart of Christianity?

If Christianity is seen as centered in Christ, what word best describes Christ to strangers as well as neighbors? Responding to that question is essential when approached by enquirers. What explains Christianity and its values from a religious, philosophical and global perspective to fellow believers & nonbelievers as well?

I recall a timely conversation during my college years on the campus of Occidental College in Los Angeles with classmates who like me brought our sandwiches from home. I couldn't afford to live on campus, and I suspect that was true for others who desired conversation together over lunch. A few young science faculty joined us also. On this particular occasion I recall the faculty members present chose to listen. Perhaps their silence was due to the question asked that day by a fellow student. She started by saying, "I can't say exactly what Christianity is, but do you see that student over there walking across the campus?" We looked and saw the student whom we all recognized. "I can't say in so many words, what Christianity is", she repeated, "but there goes a Christian. That person sums up for me my understanding what it means to be a Christian". She continued, "He is willing to accept others whatever their faults or behavior problems might be. He practices forgiveness when needed.

Of course, he also tends to be honest, a good listener, considerate, compassionate and sensitive – all fine qualities, but he goes further. He forgives and accepts others in spite of their shortcomings. That fellow student is my definition of a true believer.

Our discussion began to heat up. Would we accept this definition? How would we react to her response as we ate under the campus trees? Is "Christian forgiveness" as embodied in Jesus capture the meaning of Christianity whatever our beliefs or convictions in life might be? Would we view Christ as an exceptional example of human forgiveness for humankind? Many have heard about the wide range of disagreement among Christians regarding beliefs that cover liberal to quite conservative positions. She went on to explain her viewpoint. "To call ourselves Christians", she said, "means not only to accept God's forgiveness witnessed on the cross, but also to practice forgiving love as Jesus taught his disciples and demonstrated during his brief earthly ministry interpreted to us through our sacred texts."

Our noon discussion was reaching our time limit. Our circle of participants came from varied religious faiths and other convictions, yet we wanted to hear one another's views of Jesus in light of our own faith or philosophical positions. It was clear our discussion wasn't over in our desire to advance the common good—a task unique to every generation as we realize the interconnectedness of our lives. For me that noon discussion was another small step in life's journey unfolding the spirit of the *imago Dei*, God's image challenging us to care for one another as soulmates on the way to a fuller life.

Cindy Lou in the classic film *The Grinch* knew a lot about generosity and gift giving. No doubt many can recall that dated film as I did seeing it again recently with our grandchildren. *The Grinch* was so unacceptable and ugly to the citizens of Whoville, except for Cindy Lou, who saw possibilities in him. Both the Grinch and the village folks learned over a painful period of time to forgive and accept one another, following the example of young Cindy Lou. In real life, forgiving and being forgiven is a thin line for many within our faith or non-faith traditions. Perhaps the person who feels hurt the most ought to start the process. The heart of Christianity reveals the dynamics of forgiveness primarily as God's suffering love symbolized by the cross. Suffering love is a way of expressing forgiveness as we learn to accept others, difficult as it might be for either side of an issue. There is seemingly no forgiveness without sacrifice and pain.

This is true in every genocide among humankind. Every child, parent and grandparent have some understanding of this pain which has left scars and caused household divisions and civil wars within nations as well as between nations.

Whoever wishes to maintain healthy relationships is aware of the tensions involved. Every broken relationship stays broken until we are willing to struggle through some understanding. Forgiveness is the cleansing that starts the healing process. Unfortunately, there is often so much anger and bitterness that we may be unwilling to enter into that forgiving process. True peace and justice seem to elude humankind. We are surprisingly more comfortable with our hatred and desire to get even, so that we refuse to begin the difficult climb toward genuine forgiveness and healing. This was the Grinch's condition. He had isolated himself from everyone. Are we aware of persons living "Grinch-like" lives today? They have imprisoned themselves by their attitudes and behavior, trying to bury their fears in affluent lifestyles with disciplined civility that often lacks joy. We may utter glib remarks on cheap forgiveness in our superficial etiquette and pseudo-relationships. Let's not fool ourselves. It's unlikely for many of us to simply "forgive and forget", doubtful that we could live any better whether we worship or not on weekends.

Forgiving encounters will never wipe out the scars and the hurts of the past, but in a mysterious way the spirit of the *imago Dei* enables us to surface above the scars, helping us to initiate healing that leads to reconciliation with our gracious God, as well as with those who have harmed us. Forgiveness is like a clear, cool stream of water necessary to cleanse our long-standing wounds. And the spirit of the *imago Dei* will assist us to get started on a more fruitful pathway to a fuller life. How many loved ones are waiting right now for some family member to initiate this forgiving process? Perhaps the person who feels the most wronged should start the process of forgiveness. God gives us the courage to take the first step. A forgiving bath may need to be repeated a number of times to be truly cleansed of the tensions that have robbed us from living a fuller life, trusting God and one another.

We also need to remind ourselves that "forgive and forget" is an empty cliché; it is neither biblical nor a belief worth harboring. We are mere humans and we can never really forget the wrongs and hurts committed. The scars of broken relationships, rejection, unfairness and injustice will always be there. We need to go through the pain of learning to forgive without forgetting, discovering through suffering love to accept those who have wronged us. That is not easy. It may even seem impossible. God is aware of that reality in our lives but does not wish to see us defeated by it. We can't hide our crosses in life; they are heavy symbols to bear whatever our faith beliefs might be. God gives us the grace to bear our burdens.

151

The message of forgiving love is the most powerful force available today to dismantle violence and the miles of walls that imprison us. In every situation, walls appear to be the silent elephant in the community that consumes our time, energy and resources. The sad fact is that many of us really don't believe forgiveness is a realistic option in the world as it is. It is one of the major reasons why humankind is caught in a constant crossfire of wars throughout our international histories of hate and hell that we promote.

What would life be like without the possibility of forgiveness? *For many of us it would be hell!* Among humankind today many are now living in hell, refusing to transcend the emotional barriers of alienation. Anxieties, fears, guilt and hatred take us back to the strife between Caine and Able who also were created in *God's image.* Denying our past, does not free us from our imprisoned natures filled with greed, fear and ignorance that have eclipsed the beacon of light that could lead to a fuller life of abundance if we are willing to accept our charge and responsibility to be faithful stewards of our Creator's creation honoring our ageless God.

Our task now is to be goodwill ambassadors, addressing the expanding needs of humankind to live in peace, practicing justice and love, especially forgiving love, exemplified in the spirit of the *imago Dei* at our creation. Admittedly, it is difficult to break out of self-imposed prisons of selfishness and greed.

152

Unfortunately, it seems that those who hate together stay together, using it as their battle-cry in our conflicted communities. How much current energy and feelings are wasted daily through distrust and suspicions? *Caring for our human togetherness matters!*

Forgiveness, however, falls on deaf ears in a cynical society that stereotypes its enemy and rationalizes its own behavior. Do the unforgiving realities of our lives make lasting friendships unaffordable? Lasting friendships without forgiveness are impossible. Social loneliness is more likely. The future of Facebook and social media are limited when our hunger for privacy and trust mounts in our lives. It is a lesson from our pandemic that is embedded in us now. Will the lesson endure?

Can we go on living on our isolated mountaintop like *The Grinch*, protecting ourselves behind private fences and gated communities? Whatever the case, we won't overcome our deeper longing to belong. *Healthy relationships do matter!* Our Creator-God loves the world with a realistic awareness that forgiving relations also count. In this context Jesus befriended the unwanted of his day--the tax collectors, prostitutes and those who neglect the helpless and needy. Jesus alarmed the establishment of his day and also his own disciples with his observations. His goal was to give to all who listened a new lease on life. He invited his listeners to renew their relationships and transform their lives into becoming leaders of goodwill empowered to care for one another's communities. When Jesus was asked, how much forgiveness was required to improve lives, he replied with directness, *seventy times seven* indicating that the cost of forgiveness was priceless. *"Where there is little forgiveness, there is little love and where there is much forgiveness there is much love",* indicated Jesus. In short, forgiving one another is actually the human way of loving.

Every forgiving encounter, however, is a risky business. We may be rejected and rebuffed in our attempt to forgive. We may even be seen in the community as being too self-righteous, "holier than thou." We also run the risk of being conned. Jesus took on those risks at the cross. Many continue to play pseudo-games of faith as Jesus encountered in his day. Without taking risks in life, however, nothing is gained. Jesus took a chance and befriended the unacceptable from all corners of his society. He then told his followers to be prepared to risk and even to get burned, if necessary, to establish their authenticity as ambassadors of goodwill to further God's Will.

As a graduate doctoral student at the University of Basel in Switzerland, I recall many insightful conversations with its distinguished faculty members. On one of my regular sessions at the home of Professor Fritz Lieb, a Swiss colleague of Professor Karl Barth, we were engaged in a theological discussion. Professor Lieb made an unforgettable comment that I still remember. He said, "I hope you won't be shocked, and realize by now, that there is really only one true Christian among humans, and his name is Jesus. The rest of us unhappily are counterfeits". How would this observation be received if mentioned from the pulpit or presented at the annual congregational meeting with its yearly report? No one wishes to be a fake believer, at least not publicly. The true believer of whatever *faith* tradition according to Jesus, is revealed in his story of the "good Samaritan". Would this story bring a ring of authenticity to our discussions as we design our biblical passports on the theme of **HEAVEN'S PASSPORT for a fuller life?** Would it draw us closer to the spirit of the *imago Dei*? Is the *"good Samaritan"* example familiar among religious faiths?

Scripture to consider:
Matthew 26:69-75; also note chapter 27:46
Luke 7:40-50 and Luke 10:29-37 (The Good Samaritan story)
John 4:7-42

Books and articles for classroom and neighborhood discussions:
Hans Kung, *On Being a Christian*, Doubleday & Company, Inc., New York

John M. Barry, *Roger Williams and The Creation of the American Soul: Church, State, and the Birth of Liberty*, Viking, New York

Nicholas Kristof, *"What Religion Would Jesus Belong To?"*, *The New York Times*, September 4, 2016.

Ted Olsen, *"Is the God of Muhammad the Father of Jesus?"*, Christianity *Today*, February 4, 2002

Amy Frykholm, "Who Is Jesus For Muslims?", An interview with Islam scholar Zeki Saritoprak's on his recent book, *"Islamic Spirituality: Theology and Practice for the Modern World"*, *The Christian Century*, June 7, 2017

Peggy Levitt, *God Needs No Passport, Harvard Divinity Bulletin*, Autumn, 2006. Religious faith can be a puzzle for immigrants looking for secure anchors, as they begin life anew from their distant homelands. As goodwill ambassadors, we can provide insightful guidance to new arrivals spiritually and socially.

Jaroslav Pelikan, *Jesus Through the Centuries: His Place in the History of Culture*, Yale University Press

James Denny, *The Death of Christ*, edited by RVG Tasker, Inter-Varsity Press

Albert Schweitzer, *The Psychiatric Study of Jesus: Exposition and Criticism*, The Beacon Press.

Michael Gerson, *"How Evangelicals Lost Their Way and Got Hooked by Donald Trump"*, *The Atlantic*, April

2018. Gerson is known both as an evangelical and respected reporter for *The Washington Post*.

Chapter 13. Can We Escape from Suffering?

Based on our life experiences wherever we live, we have been exposed to human suffering since birth. Much of our suffering today has been reduced with progress in medical health care, however it isn't always affordable to everyone in need of advanced skills and equipment.

Another major concern for humankind today is the excessive use of carbon and oil products harming our natural resources and threatening us with climate-warming dangers everywhere. Knowledgeable experts with growing evidence seek collective action from world leaders **to act now** in the best interests of their citizens before it is too late to correct the situation! See the timely article by Richard Schiffman, *"Pandemic? Lab Says Main Crisis Is Still Climate", New York Times* (4/26/20). The challenge before us is serious; any further delay based on political and economic self-interests is unwise and can be globally unfortunate for everyone. The situation calls for us to act as a concerned family of nations united in a common effort to avoid serious suffering later. Hopefully we have learned some lessons from our recent pandemic-COVID-19 crisis. It seems the majority of the global population then had not been sufficiently informed of what was at stake for them nor equipped with adequate resources needed to save lives.

The forces of nature require greater attention and stewardship from citizens everywhere working together to supersede any single nation's self-interest for the good of all, upholding the spirit of the *imago Dei*. We would be failing our mission to our Creator-God otherwise. Our highest priority is to pay attention to our common stewardship uniting heaven and earth honoring the wonders of creation (which includes our lives as well) to the glory of God. Unfortunately, our human history with its wars, plagues and poorly handled pandemics that reveals human shortcomings and self-interests at the high cost of human lives that bypasses the spirit of the *imago Dei,* making it almost impossible to keep human life human, having lost interest it seems in the common good. Have we also misinterpreted purposefully the stories from our sacred texts? As we return to our scriptural stories discussing our biblical passports, we need to refocus on God's beacon of light in our darkness leading us to fulfill our true stewardship of goodwill on behalf of God's creation everywhere.

None of us in our suffering are prevented from praying that God's grace might still extend to those in need in spite of our wrongs against humanity and the dangers to created life and the climate that nurtures us. At times, the outcome from our prayers may not be as we wish, Jesus was well aware of these conditions from his own cross, but there is also the experience of inner peace that continues to uphold us in the mystery of our suffering. The ripple effect of 9/11 upon Americans was felt across the country and among citizens around the world who still remember the price many families have paid on their soil. Global complexity and distrust still continues, however, to return among the newly wounded since 9/11 in families now numbered in the world's circle of suffering lives. *None of us can really escape from suffering, we all are in need of compassion.*

Perhaps this is why many of us continue to watch television stories and films that show their wounds on their bodies among today's displaced minorities as well as the many stories from yesterday's unhealed wounds of injustice remaining from slavery, indenture, and unjust practices known to immigrants many of whom were victims of genocide. We are all making efforts to build trust among each other, while realizing that distrust remains under our skins regardless of how our culture was classified.

The forces of fear and hunger are always a challenge whether walking or driving on our streets and parks. How welcoming are we in discerning God's Will as to whether or not we should reach out to strangers on the road, worried perhaps that we might be conned in the

161

process? How should we react in our urban oriented lives? Do we believe that every stranger has a *social virus* and that we should simply move on, feeling guilty perhaps as we rationalize our fearful behavior?

Some of us continue to search for a more ideal community where diversity is minimized, and fears are less visible. Others desire more adventure in life, looking for some highway to outer space that would take us to an exceptional planet free of worries and filled with fun without any suffering. We might also consider the heavens above, according to calculations made by astronomers at the University of British Columbia there could be as many as 6 billion earthlike planets in our galaxy. (UBS *Science*, June 16) Is that the kind of exceptional world we are currently hoping to find? Will that be paradise for us? Or do wish to be lured (or pulled) by some adventuresome unseen magnetic force into a black hole?

Perhaps there is an exceptional world in space not yet fully discovered or developed. For now, I believe there is more promise in outlining one's biblical passport to envision a fuller life as ambassadors of goodwill fulfilling God's ends in the spirit of the *imago Dei,* enabling us to experience a safer and saner planet with *Heaven's Passport directing us to a fuller life on earth,* with heighten curiosity to explore the universe as soul-mates and stewards of our Creator-God.

In a recent issue of *Foreign Affairs*, July/August 2018 published by the *Council of Foreign Affairs,* six worlds are discussed as possibilities for humans. Which of these worlds would we prefer: (1) a realist world where the players change, but the actual war games remain, (2) a liberal world seen as a resilient order with progressive gods, (3) a tribal world where group identity is everything, (4) a Marxist world with continued mistrust of capitalism, (5) a tech world willing to invest in a digital revolution undermining one's privacy, (6) or a warming world where climate change matters to humans more than anything else? Missing in the *Foreign Affairs* list of worlds is (7) a spiritual world based on people's faith organized around today's major religions on earth. A spiritual world, no doubt would be questioned by skeptical powerbrokers influenced by military power and international business interests. Whatever the case, today's "spiritual world" of followers consists of millions upon millions of lives that can't be overlooked. These believers with their respective visions when together in spirit can create their own understanding of "spiritual power" for their followers as they uncover common values upheld by their Creator-God. They will honor humankind together as a spiritual force to further *God's Will* for all created life that can result in our *common good* leading to *peace, justice, goodwill and abundance for all. This kind of partnership as stewardship is biblically embedded in seeking **God's Will, not ours**, and witness the difference in the quality of our lives in partnership with our Creator-God.*

Suffering Also Offers Lessons in Courage & Hope:
The Apostle Paul inspired persons in his School of Suffering with his own *"thorn in the flesh"* and its mounting pain as he cried out to God for help! Had God forsaken him? Do worthy lessons come from suffering? No doubt his own suffering was a humbling experience that also strengthened him in ministry as his epistles (letters) indicated from followers and his students throughout the centuries. His suffering also served as a means to humanize his needs to the emerging congregations and authorities he encountered in travels throughout the Greek Orient of his day. I wonder at times if Paul fully realized the ways in which suffering empowered him in his new role as a goodwill ambassador to others carrying out God's purposes, as he embraced the Jesus he had opposed earlier in his life. Before Paul completed his new mission in life, he became more mindful that suffering connected him to God's love and grace and strengthened his authenticity with strangers on his journey to Rome. Before we think of following Paul's understanding of suffering, consider the following points.

First, we need to admit that there are many forms of suffering such as **physical suffering** from starvation, harassment, terminal illness, genetic disorders, drug problems, etc. We have made progress in alleviating many forms of physical suffering, but physical pain will always exist and challenge our sensitivities, drowning individuals and families into untold tears of despair. No matter how hard we pray, the "thorn in our flesh" remains. This thorn has material and economic aspects as well: loss of employment, housing, possessions, safety needs and piling debts at home that contributes to our psychic and physical suffering.

Second, there is **philosophical and religious suffering** as we struggle with the meaning of life, seeking answers oftentimes to unanswerable questions, "What can I know? What ought I to do? What may I hope for?" Persons everywhere, including members of religious communities, wrestle and suffer in anguish over these questions at every major junction in our lives. Everyone's faith journey seeks certitudes that we cannot defend dogmatically. Instead we need to confess truthfully there is no perfect theological statement that confronts the mystery and strangeness that occurs in life. Everyone's faith journey is a humbling process. As we defend our "dogmatic theologies", let's not lose sight of the fact that our knowledge is limited during the course of our lifetime. This includes our dogmas as well. We may also outgrow some answers we currently hold tightly within us, as our faith deepens which happened to Jacob and Job in their prayers and encounters with God as told in our sacred texts.

In our spiritual suffering, we discover that living faith in God is actually beyond our complete comprehension. Implicit in the very nature of authentic faith is this sense of incompleteness. That is what Jesus was trying to teach the "doubting Thomas" that resides within each of us. It is also why Jesus often taught in parables to his followers and disciples. Our questions in life are left with commas, semicolons, but not necessarily with periods that end our reflections in these matters. Our quest for knowledge extends beyond our lifetime as we reach out to eternity.

Third, there is **psychological suffering** as we increasingly realize that no matter how street smart and intelligent, we are, we still need emotional intelligence to function in a caring and loving way in a society of broken relationships. Every broken relationship – divine and human – creates emptiness and darkness within us, leading at times to that dark night of the soul with depressed feelings. Maintaining psychic health in a dysfunctional society can in itself be a suffering experience, complicated by larger issues like 9/11 or a pandemic crisis that drives us closer to the edges of our hellish feelings. Our insights lead us to realize how helpless we feel to "fix things", but how essential it is nevertheless, to be there for others when needed. Seminary and medical graduates are oftentimes, like Job's friends, bent on giving advice and answers when the real need is simply to be a listening ear, backed by the reassurance that God's Spirit will guide us to listen well and speak briefly.

Fourth, there is also **political suffering** when we often blame others for our ills. These "other groups" may be ethnic, racial, economic or gender-oriented and are perceived as the "enemy" the cause of one's illness or the nation's mistakes. From such biased attitudes "political action" is organized "to correct" the situation. Such action often leads to unfair suffering for those targeted groups (Armenians, Jews, Syrians, Muslims, Arabs, Latinos, Indians, and Asians, etc.) resulting in genocides and holocausts. Genocidal activities were widely practiced in the 20th Century and unfortunately continue into our 21st century. A post-9/11 world must be leery of collective fault-finding as "the solution" to suffering; when confronting contemporary complexity, today's suffering may suggest that "the enemy" wears many disguises whether seen on Facebook or reported as some kind of conspiracy.

In all these known and unknown dimensions of suffering, our response as individuals and religious institutions will increase or impede political suffering. A reconciling interfaith approach containing a mixture of nationalistic biases may benefit humankind, if the underlying motivation is to uphold the *imago Dei* with humility, acting wisely to resolve issues before us.

A collective outlook of religious hope can spark an enlightened desire for personal growth, transforming support groups within our religious institutions and also schools and community centers where learning about the *imago Dei*, affirms humankind's importance to all in the community. We can be a fellowship of sufferers learning to support each other through our respective journeys of faith with the collective wisdom of the ages surrounding us with meaningful conversations that adds to our understanding as we confront the storms of life h gaining some helpful insights from the experiences of others before us. Paul in his epistles calls us to rejoice in our suffering, knowing that it leads to a healing pathway exceeding our expectations. Ponder in your quiet moments Paul's wisdom, "to boast in our sufferings, because suffering produces perseverance, which produces character, and character leads to hope, and hope does not disappoint us, because it is sustained by God's Spirit of love fulfilling us." (Romans 5:3-5).

This has been my observation knowing that spiritual growth always involves pain, and pain in turn is often accompanied by the question, "Why me?" My grandsons Caleb, Luke and Christian have been asking that question recently since they were all graduating from their respective universities and Christian from high school without their traditional graduation programs that includes parents and grandparents. In particular, they were asking, "Why did COVID-19 crisis happen now, preventing us from having our graduations as expected?"

At times, I suspect that recent seminarians graduating are probably wondering if their studies in philosophy and theology have simply raised more questions than answers as they consider their next steps in life. Is educated learning simply a process of discovering in depth our ignorance at higher levels of abstraction without satisfactory answers. At other times, I realize that none of us escapes entirely from suffering with unanswered or incomplete answers to life's timeless question, *"Why?"* asked often at disappointing moments in our lives.

I suspect we are all born to be students—to ask a lifetime of questions, gaining partial answers during our journeys in life. Does our questioning finally end with death? Every graduation event focuses on these puzzling questions, directing us onward in unexpected ways. Actually, our lives are filled with commas and semi colons, and our final periods come much later on God's calendar filled with graceful notes based on our sacred texts. With time, we come to realize that our most helpful prayers direct us to fulfill *God's Will, not ours.* In the end, we discover it that it is far better and wiser when God is given the last word throughout our journeys in life. The Apostle Paul expresses it best in his first epistle to the Corinthians. (Chapter13: 8-13)
This is Professor Peterson's contemporary translation of that sacred text from ***The Message: The Bible in Contemporary Language:***

> *"We don't yet see things clearly. We're squinting in a fog, peering through a mist. But it won't be long before the weather clears, and the sun shines bright! We'll see it all then, see it all as clearly as God sees us, knowing him directly just as he knows us!*

But for right now, until that completeness, we have three things to do to lead us toward that consummation. Trust steadily in God, hope unswervingly, love extravagantly. And the best of the three is love."

Scripture to consider:
Genesis 11:1-9
Book of Job read in its entirety.
Psalm 90, 130, & 138
Proverbs 3
Ecclesiastes 7 (See Peterson's translation- "Don't Take Anything for Granted)
Matthew13&14 Read from two versions (e.g. NRSV &The Message)
Romans 5:3-5
I Corinthians 13:8-13 (Paul's quote at the end of this chapter.)
II Corinthians 12:1-10

Articles and books for discussions:
Samuel Wells writes on the logic of forgiveness entitled, *"A Friend Like Peter", The Christian Century,* February 6, 2007. Wells also wrote in *The Century, Is Love Stronger?* April 25, 2018 *"In the worst of times, if you have a choice between false hope and truth, share the truth—love is stronger than death."* Another Wells' article is *"Liturgy at the edge of life",* February 27, 2019. He offers a timely funeral service for those affected by suicide. See also Erika Andersen

observation, *"Is God the Answer to the Suicide Epidemic?"*, *The Wall Street Journal, July 12, 20019*

Also read a pandemic case reported by Nicholas Kristof, *"A Young Doctor, Fighting for His Life"*, a case study of a hero saving the lives of others in the pandemic crisis needs to fight for his own life as well, *The New York Times*, May 5, 2020

Bethany Sollereder, *"From Survival to Love: Evolution and the Problem of Suffering"*, *The Christian Century,* September 17, 2014. Sollereder is inspired by Andrew Elphinstone, *Freedom, Suffering and Love,* London, SCM Press

Time Magazine, March 2, 2012 had a striking article on opioids with photographs by James Nachtwey. The excess use of opioids has caused much suffering for users and families throughout our global society.

The following are other aspects of suffering—beginning with Paul Kalanithi, a neurosurgeon who died of stage IV cancer in March 2015. He had so much to live for. His lost life numbs many with unanswered questions raised from his modest book, *"When Breath Becomes Air"*, Random House, New York

Brett McGurk, *"The Father I Never Forgave"*, *New York Times*, May 3, 2020

Stuart Blume, "The Global Fight Over Vaccines", New York Times, May 3, 2020

Kate Bowler, *Everything Happens for A Reason: And Other Lies I've Loved,* Random House, New York. This started as a study on hope in the midst of suffering and tragedy as preached by those she nicknamed as the "prosperity gospel" followers. Bowler, an assistant professor at Duke Divinity School, discovered at the age of 35 that she was unfortunately diagnosed with Stage IV colon cancer. Our prayers for God's grace are with her and her circle of family and friends.

Alisa Roth, *INSANE: America's Criminal Treatment of Mental Illness,* Basic Books Amulet & Shane Bauer, *AMERICAN PRISON: A Reporter's Undercover Journey into the Business of Punishment,* Penguin, NY

Chapter 14. How Does the Bible Understand Success?

I remember a conversation with an Oxy (Occidental College) classmate and longtime friend Merrill about his expectations for his growing children. He surprised me by saying that he had left his church and pulled his children out of Sunday School. When I asked why, he replied, "It seems that almost everything we hear from the pulpit and even in the Sunday School classes are against success. I want to succeed, and I also expect my children to be successful. The church ought to reinforce that message."

"Wait a minute," I recall answering him, "How do we understand success?" Are we simply defining success as the absence of failure? Certainly, our culture has taught us that success and failure are interchangeable conditions depending on the trade-offs involved. At times the price we pay for success is too high, and in retrospect we know we have failed in the midst of success. Those who have been in such a spot, know what I mean. Warren Buffett, a hero to many investors reminded the public during the pandemic crisis that

173

many businesses took large financial losses, with no guaranteed assurances of success. The complexities of life's realities can't be ignored; we need to face up to possible errors and the feeling of nakedness when the tide is out, but we aren't alone in the situation. Scripture sums it up with a reflective question saying, *"What shall it profit us to gain the whole world and forfeit our lives? Or what can we give in exchange for our souls?"* (Mark 8: 34-38) The high cost of falling apart in an pandemic crisis reveals a larger picture of neglect within the structures of our society that may be more serious than our financial setbacks. We need a renewal of relationships on all levels of our society.

I was traveling to Los Angeles to give a lecture and attend a retreat for church leaders. Before these events started, Doris and I on our arrival at LAX, hurried to meet old friends for a dinner party. These friends were high achievers by most measurements. One business executive surprised me with question, asking how much time was required of me to prepare a successful sermon? His question surprised me, but I knew that the word "success" was important in his vocabulary. I responded by indicating that it was difficult to say, since I'm working directly and indirectly on a sermon all the time. It seems we all have active ideas and imaginations that never rest, we are constantly in motion whenever we are engage with others working on a project or preparing future sermons. Usually, I find that one sermon delivered can be many different sermons received depending on the listener's circumstances at that time.

I went on to say that I was presently working on a sermon focused on the question of success. There seems to be confusion between our secular and spiritual understandings of success in our culture today. Is worldly success different from spiritual success? If so, why do religious institutions seem to measure success by worldly standards? I proceeded then to invite everyone around the dinner table to assist me in clarifying my thoughts by participating in my homework as I continued to reflect on my sermon. Although this particular dinner conversation took place some time ago, I am still reminded of it today by our California friends at more recent get-togethers.

Several definitions of success emerged from our dinner conversation. Most felt that there was no such thing as *"Christian success"*. Success was simply success, and you can't argue with success whatever its measurements might be past or present. In any given situation we need to recognize our varied contexts when reflecting and measuring the meaning of success and to update our definitions.

Here is a sampling of the responses I recall from that evening:

First, several felt strongly that success was measured by how one's children developed. It seems parents often feel they have succeeded or failed in life as measured by their children's accomplishments. Parents often feel they have done a successful job if their offspring are financially independent.

Second, others mentioned that success is measured by one's savings or net worth. *Forbes* and *Fortune* certainly make us aware with their annual list of the wealthiest in society wherever they are and how it happened.

Third, someone said success is basically service to others; willingness to be of help. Yet some honestly confessed they were exhausted with helping others.

Fourth, another dinner guest said success is living in simplicity with elegance – "None of this trashy consumption is acceptable to me," she remarked.

Fifth, someone said success is status, influence and power in the community, state and nation. Given that most of us present shared a common American-Armenian heritage, the following two examples were mentioned a number of times: former California governor George Deukmejian and his outstanding efforts to unite political parties in the state, and Kirk Kerkorian from the business world who used much of his financial success to help those in need, in spite of his business concerns and family challenges faced in his lifetime.

Sixth, success for another was simply learning to accept and be honest with oneself, a personal sense of contentment, a quality of life often lacking in social relationships.

Seventh, finally someone said, success is a matter of sheer accident or good fortune. It's having sold your stocks prior to the last major downturn. It's having a lucky number at a lottery contest. Some were wondering, whether we had already become a lottery-minded society whose lives are measured by accident or chance? Have our friends defined success as persons would understand it today?

Perhaps conversations of this nature might be by-passed in our discussion groups as we design our biblical passports, until we know each other better. For a number of years at Pittsburgh Seminary we sponsored a Clergy/Business Forum with a monthly downtown breakfast gathering. For a series of gatherings, we discussed various models and images of success in our global society. A chief executive officer in our group kicked off the initial discussion with a critique of Lee Iacocca, former CEO of Chrysler Motor Company. During his period in the company's history, Iacocca and Chrysler were synonymous. He is credited with the dramatic turnaround of that company inspired by his leadership. Would Iacocca be seen as a model of success today? Is the saving of a corporation, providing jobs for thousands and making a return on equity for shareholders admired currently? Is the measurement of success in a business-oriented society solely a quantitative matter? The bottom-line, of course, is important, and so is the equitable distribution of earnings to employees, investors and the community.

Another model of success discussed by our Clergy/Business Forum was led by a medical doctor/hospital executive. His subject that morning was Mother Teresa. She has certainly been heralded as a "successful modern saint" and was the recipient of the 1979 Nobel Prize for Peace, a sign of having arrived in our global society. Would we concur that Mother Teresa's devotion to the poor and the dying, along with her simple lifestyle is remarkable? Would she also be our model of true success? I suspect Mother Teresa's example, while widely respected, is actually intimidating for many, who can't quite concur that her lifestyle would be their choice. Mother Teresa isn't found on their roadmap to success.

A third model of success discussed by our breakfast group was led by the owner of a privately held company. He began with a degree of humility by confessing that the most important gift handed to him was watching his father direct the business with integrity. The modest business he inherited has now been greatly expanded. Success for this man, however, was not so much the growth of his business, as it was learning to bring his life under control. Success for him has been learning to manage his life. How many of us wish that we felt less victimized by the day-in and day-out events which control us? Success for many is taking charge of our calendars rather than being dictated by endless interruptions and deadlines. Many really don't envy having a leadership position in any organization, institution nor do they seek an elected office in government. I have also known colleagues as faculty members who are quite content not to be burdened with the responsibilities of being a seminary president.

As believers and nonbelievers, we all have our respective views of success in life. Our Bibles surprisingly say very little directly on success. In Joshua 1:6-9 we have a clue to a biblical understanding of success. God informs Joshua that the Israelites will be able to claim the Promised Land successfully, if they are faithfully obedient to God's command. The basis for our biblical understanding of success is centered on doing God's *Will, instead of our own*. There is indeed a Promised Land for everyone to claim when we are truly faithful. Unfortunately, most settle for secondary pieces of real estate in our lives, since we are unwilling to pursue with any degree of tenacity and urgency God's higher vision, which might not be the "promised-land" of our own choice. There can be a difference between God's plan and our outlook channeled by self-interests. As we design our biblical passports, hopefully we will be open for suggestions from questions heard while seeking an understanding of God's Will embedded in the spirit of the *imago Dei*. We need to be open for honest dialogue in building trust that sustains relationships of peace, justice & abundance as we enjoy

God's creation in our journeys as soul-mates embedded in *God's image,* the *imago Dei.*

I was invited to Washington D.C to be with fellow pastors by the late Senator Mark Hatfield of Oregon when Mother Teresa was visiting the nation's capital. The Senator asked Mother Teresa how she kept going, since there appeared to be so little success in her battle to alleviate suffering among the poor and dying in Calcutta. She responded by saying, "Mr. Hatfield, God has called me not to be successful, but to faithfully obey the vision of God's Kingdom revealed to me". A believer's view of spiritual success always begins with our divine commitment of faithfulness, as we submit ourselves to God's calendar and direction daily, fulfilling the *imago Dei* as the People of God, faithfully serving diverse gatherings when asked as ambassadors of goodwill fulfilling *God's Will* in our lives.

Those who have read Iacocca's *Autobiography* will recall in the opening pages his description of being fired by Henry Ford as president of the Ford Motor Company. He acknowledges the humiliation that it caused him and his family, and consequently he says he would never be able to forgive Mr. Ford. It is precisely at this point that the "successful Iacocca" may have failed from a biblical perspective. Entering into that forgiving and humbling process regardless how difficult is basic to every believer's true identity.

Being successful is an on-going process for believers. Scripture informs us that Abraham was a friend of God, and herein resides the success of his leadership. Friendship with God comes through disciplined study, prayer and Spirit-led engagement to further the Kingdom of God. Trust in God invites believers to follow up with trusting relationships with others, indicating our common need to practice forgiving love with caring concern, in spite of the mess we may have caused in broken relationships and misspoken comments. This requires a mutual cleaning up, freeing ourselves from our towers of babble and opening the gates of separation, acting as goodwill ambassadors to improve lives across borders, giving thanks to our Creator-God whose abundance we can enjoy mutually when peace and justice are in place.

In short, we need to be guided by God's calendar, free of our biases and self-interests. God is not to be blamed for our nearsighted choices; we need to correct our vision to see more fully the rainbow of hope ahead. Loyalty can't be bought in the trade-offs we often demand. God's wisdom when applied with humility will take us further according to our sacred texts. We have learned from experience to be suspicious of those who shower us with gifts. Neither should we say, "I trust in God, but refuse to trust anyone else", even though we have been burned often by empty promises, leaving us stuck in the mud creating nightmares for ourselves.

Returning to Augustine's prayer offered centuries ago is relevant, "Our hearts are restless until they rest in God". Our biblical passports, which I refer to as *"Heaven's Passport"* will hopefully lead us to higher ground and a fuller life by God's grace. The essential lesson to remember is clear--God refuses to place a price on our souls; why then are we willing to settle for less? (Matthew 4:1-11 & Mark 8:34-9:1)

Scripture to consider:
Proverbs 3:5-6
Joshua 1:6-9
Luke 9:23-27
James 5:1-20
Acts 17:16-31 (Paul at the Areopagus with Athenians to discuss the 'unknown god')

Books and articles for classroom and neighborhood discussions:
Harvey Cox, "When Jesus Came to Harvard", Houghton Mifflin, Boston

David Brooks, *The Road to Character*, Random House, New York

John W. Gardner, *On Leadership,* The Free Press, New York

Michael J. Sandel, *Justice: What's the Right Thing to Do?* Farrar, Straus And Giroux, New York

Drew Gilpin Faust, *THIS REPUBLIC OF SUFFERING: Death and The American Civil War*, Alfred A. Knopf. Professor Faust of Harvard University states that approximately 620,000 soldiers plus civilians were killed in the Civil War.

Michael Maccoby, *"Trust Is Also the Business of Business"*, *NYTimes*, March 31, 1978. Group, P.C.

Kenneth E. Goodpaster and John B. Matthews, Jr., *"CAN A CORPORATION HAVE A CONSCIENCE?"*, *Harvard Business Review* Vol. 60, No.1, Jan.-Feb. 1982.

Robert B. Reich, *THE COMMON GOOD*, Alfred A. Knopf, New York

Jon Meacham, *The Soul of America: The Battle for Our Better Angels*, Random House, New York

Adam Cohen, *Supreme Inequality: The Supreme Court's Fifty-Year Battle for A More Unjust America*, Penguin Press, New York

Edward Felsenthal, Editor-in-Chief & CEO of *TIME* has committed the July 6-13, 2020 issue to the theme— *AMERICA MUST CHANGE* which is a timely topic for classroom & neighborhood discussions as we prepare our individual biblical passports.

Part V: Disclose Mistakes

Chapter 15. Has an *Apocalypse* Begun?

The unending task for educational and religious institutions is to stay alert in a rapidly changing world. Our latest pandemic-COVID-19 has placed apocalyptic fears before us. With the lockdown cautiously being lifted while medical personnel and leaders still warn us to maintain social distancing, it has been amazing how educational and religious institutions have shifted to remote teaching and worship services, alert to changes that could actually draw us closer together. In short, most of us are desiring to be current, faithful, and awake as our responsibilities increase. In cases where this is happening, individuals find themselves more engaged now than ever in the welfare of humankind. Citizens of goodwill around the world are being challenged to apply their skills to promote peace and understanding within their communities, realizing that any climate apocalypse emerging could also raise a host of other fears-pandemic or nuclear-igniting global fires endangering the wellbeing of creation.

The late columnist Charles Krauthammer of *The Washington Post* had his own personal apocalypse with a tragic accident at his university's swimming pool which almost ended his life. He was crippled for a lifetime. His moments of despair and deep discernment over his condition led him to write, "when people stop believing in God, they will believe in anything— totalitarianisms of all sorts--if atheism is (God forbid) true, it is dangerous. It leads to utter desolation". Irwin Stelze recalled these remarks of Krauthammer in his article in *The Wall Street Journal,* June 22, 2018, honoring the memory of Krauthammer's life.

From our sacred texts, we learn that major apocalypses were associated with divine displeasure of human behavior which sidetracks creation and dismisses God's purposes. In this nuclear age we continue to cast shadows of insecurity, realizing that we can't escape our responsibility for creating atomic or nuclear explosions that will be further compounded with climatic changes leading perhaps to other apocalypses. We have become increasingly nearsighted as we promote our will against God's farsighted vision to benefit humankind's stewardship *for a fuller life on earth with* **Heaven's Passport**. God expects us to transform our communities into creative nations that promise peace, hope and prosperity in our partnerships of goodwill with each other, embedded as we are with the *imago Dei.*
Unfortunately, it appears we have lost that singular vision. (Ecclesiastes 7:29) Nation and racial wars promote many visions as each side seeks to outlast the other. We are simply out of balance, as each side

envisions its own kingdom and success. Many flags are flown to identify our diverse loyalties backed by our religious symbols, with added words for a national pledge or motto. This can be exciting in Olympic sports, but a disaster when words can kill millions in wars represented by our national flags & mottos. We try to balance the situation globally with international business trade looking after our self-interests and success within our rankings among nations. The world markets are now asking if global business interests should take such priority over domestic interests in our interconnected and interdependent world. Today's politics on the internet confuses us: handshakes and trade-wars are also insufficient means for building trust among nations as seen recently in the British/European Union (EU) split across borders and its questionable impact around the world. Aren't we all questioning poverty and displaced lives knocking down borders to escape dehumanizing regimes? Actually, we need to stop blaming others for our failings. We must avoid "blaming games" that are essentially unproductive, simply adding fear and loss of confidence among us. Skeptics dismiss totally the spirit of the *imago Dei* thinking that global stewardship of creation under God's inspiration as being essentially unrealistic today. Instead, the politics of self-interests prevails among nations influenced to invest along with their powerbrokers to back the ***religion of realpolitik***.

Every nation large or small has national pride—a sense of its own uniqueness or exceptionalism, but an insufficient grasp of collective greatness to enhance global peacemaking. Polite relations without depth are inadequate in a rapidly changing world interconnected with a youth culture dismayed by leaders with limited vision for the future. Today's aimless pride leaves behind a trail of discontentment and confusion as to what is meaningful in reaching out to interconnected lives desiring peace, justice, prosperity, and goodwill. The spirit of *imago Dei* among believers and seekers in their diverse cultures looks for hope able to transform lives and fulfills the wishes of our Creator-God turning us into soul-mates working for a fuller life under God's grace and love.

For now, we need to be alerted to the self-proclaimed apocalypses increasing today's fears and anxieties, and re-focus ourselves with a fresh perspective and true values in sync with ***HEAVEN'S PASSPORT: for a fuller life on earth.*** Most of us wish to live in communities that welcome not only diversity, but a sense of curiosity to learn and expand our world and deepen our faiths. Our contacts together can become the building blocks in shaping life goals and beliefs influenced by our sacred texts, learned readings, and countless discussions that shape the cornerstone of our lives and ethics in our daily relationships with each other in person or online. Our aim is to be faithful and empowered as we serve God's purposes of goodwill that challenges us daily to be faithful to our Creator-God.

A Mini-Apocalyptic at Sea:

Apocalyptic language is being more widely discussed in some quarters as we witness climate catastrophes on social media. Doris and I had a "mini-apocalyptic experience" at sea on the way to Antarctica. I was one of the chaplains for the passengers and crew departing from Florida for a two-month educational cruise around South America. An unexpected hurricane/typhoon struck the ship with vehemence hours after leaving left the southern tip of Argentina to approach Antarctica. Doris and I were sitting in the ship's library. I was preparing the next Sunday Worship Service when we experienced two huge eighty foot waves strike the ship within less than a minute of each other. Books came flying, tables were overturned and we with them. What a frightening experience! The ship felt like a cork bobbing among the huge waves as the dedicated captain and crew carefully repositioned the ship and returned to port, a considerable distance away.

As life continues, many disasters shake us, our families, and acquaintances as we face many phases of growth, expansion, and later downsizing as we age. We were surprised by the difficult emotions of "letting go" of our many collections. I had thousands of books I treasured in my personal library which I donated to schools and colleagues in ministry. Of course, there is some measure of pain in giving away what has been dear to us. On the lighter side, we survive and are liberated from the burden of possessions that prevents new experiences. In short, downsizing can be measured as the positive side of an "apocalypse".

I have shared this outlook because Doris and I have recently moved from Pittsburgh, Pennsylvania to Evanston, Illinois to be nearer to family members, transforming our lifestyle after thirty-six fulfilling years in Pittsburgh along with our previous years in Dubuque, Iowa. We have been truly blessed with significant friendships throughout our lifetime, in the U.S.A. and abroad. Friendship is important as our Creator-God intended. No doubt the topic of friendship will surface in our conversations as we plan our biblical passports.

For our growing family, departing from Dubuque to Pittsburgh was our first major move as a total family with three children—our youngest was born in Dubuque and the older two in Pasadena, California and Basel, Switzerland. The family move to Pittsburgh came when I was asked to accept the presidency and professorship at Pittsburgh Theological Seminary. When we first arrived in Pittsburgh, my focus was on the big shift from a smaller to a larger community as our family experienced the difference in size between Dubuque and Pittsburgh. Pittsburgh had recently undergone a series of regional financial setbacks, including the sharp decline of the steel industry.

Our family soon learned more about *"the Pittsburgh Apocalypse"* and its lengthy process of recovery, which was adjusting to a rebirth of hope with keen ambition to succeed. The actual major changes in Pittsburgh over our three decades there, were larger than citizens of the region had anticipated. I wonder at times today, what it would be like for recent university and college graduates from declining and displaced communities to consider returning to their home base. This was a question facing the young people of Pittsburgh in 1981 even though the sooty environment had been corrected. New expansion opportunities began through the universities, colleges and seminaries in the area. Technological advances in many areas of industry created new employment in computer and medical technologies that have gained national and international attention. A new Pittsburgh unfolded in recent decades, offering new hope along with its recognized national sports teams and its civil, educational, business and religious leadership that communicates well with one another. It takes a team spirit to rebuild a community, just as it takes a family-village to raise a child. The expansion of Artificial Intelligence (AI) currently indicates that even newer opportunities will open in Pittsburgh and elsewhere. You might read David Brooks, *"How A.I. Can Save Your Life"*, *The York Times,* June 25, 2019. Change itself often threatens us in matters of governance, worship, and relationships. Each time there is conflict, we need to step back to see if we are in sync with current wisdom and curiosity that characterizes progress as benefiting humankind oftentimes. However, making one's country great again at the expense of other countries may not seem to be the wisest motto to promote within a needy global society.

No doubt there will be greater emphasis in the future on travel in space and remote areas globally to better acquainted with our changing world and its true needs. Distrust among competing international interests in space as well as on earth might defer promised cooperative operations. An interconnected universe requires safety, privacy and the beneficial use of supply centers built jointly by countries to promote mutual use in space and in remote areas expanding tomorrow's world, and uncovering the wonders of our Creator's universe with its beauty and surprises.

Becoming a Presentologist
According to the late Russell L. Ackoff, emeritus professor and sociologist at the University of Pennsylvania, *"The future is created by what we do now. Now is the only time in which we can act. We can all be considered as presentologists, not futurologists.* Our future state will be more a product of what we do now rather than of what is done to us."* (Remarks by Professor Ackoff at Tallberg Forum on July 31, 2005.)

Professor Ackoff was among a number of speakers at the 25th anniversary of the Tallberg Forum in Sweden. I was fortunate to be among the 400-plus invited participants representing a wide assortment of professional and government officials from seventy countries throughout the world, on the theme, *"How on Earth Can We Live Together? Exploring Frameworks for Sustainable Global Interdependence"*. The Tallberg

Forum also celebrated the 100th anniversary of Dag Hammarskjold and the 60th anniversary of the United Nations founding in 1945, where Dr. Hammarskjold served as the second Secretary-General (1953-1961) of the United Nations until his untimely plane crash in Africa. The year 2005 also marked the 25th anniversary of the Peacemaking Program of the Presbyterian Church (USA) and the 60th anniversary of the atomic bombing in Hiroshima, Japan. Anniversaries with their histories seemed to be on everyone's minds then as a measurement of our limited progress globally, nationally and locally for the betterment of humankind in matters of peacemaking, justice, and everyone's wellbeing. It is now 75 years since America's soil in New Mexico experienced an atomic attack on July 16, 1945 testing the detonation of a "gadget" known then as the "Trinity bomb" enabling us to understand the impact of a nuclear disaster. (See Joshua Wheeler's article, *"When America Bombed Itself", The New York Times,* July 16, 2020.)

Perhaps the major topic that continues to deserve national and international attention today is our unspoken wish to wake up some morning envisioning God's completion of creation and now inviting us to participate in its abundant fruits with rest of humankind, as we re-read the sacred texts of Genesis informing us that humanity was embedded in the spirit of the of the *imago Dei,* inspiring us to be soul-mates caring for each other as we promote peace, justice and hope as social building blocks for communities and nations to thrive.

As it has turned out in the history of humankind such social wellbeing has sadly been uneven as long as we can remember in our uneven status causing national histories to be less realistic or just in their collective self-understanding of themselves. From such outlooks, the need became evident decades ago to have Tallberg-like events to challenge us globally to do better for the sake of humankind everywhere.

Here we are in 2020 still striving with the citizens of the world to realize the destiny our Creator-God intended for us embedded in the *imago Dei which is not yet a fully realized status in our everyday lives as humans.* What is preventing us from becoming soul-mates to each other? Why has our distrust among nations decreased with all the hopes we have had for each other? Why are we unable to trade with each other more fairly? *Is greed and distrust among us the key problem?* If so, how is every nation, large and small, as well as rich and poor, contributing to the problem and what can each do to improve the situation starting at home in our backyards and apartments? Are we too preoccupied with our own problems--personal, financial and connected to our national rankings, that our citizens are no longer able to think in terms of *the common good.* Their participation to improve our global society is too impersonal and distant. And talented citizens within nations tend to be too critical and underappreciated by leaders in powers that any progress is tasteless and restricted. Market rankings among nations can become the unseen roots behind our forever wars that have divided nations between haves and have-nots in very unhealthy ways. ***What justification does marketplace ranking have in a needy world?*** *Actually,* competition can give zest to our lives, especially when we are engaged in fair competition that nurtures healthy and honest sports, builds businesses for the welfare of its citizens and educational awards that provides incentives to parents as well as their children, etc. Most trading wars it seems undermines useful competition and meaningful jobs, and with time actually destroys the outcome of any gain claimed. Are we too late to realize the difference between wise and unwise competition in today's global marketplace?

Do we need to remind ourselves, that the forces dehumanizing our lives are pushing us toward forms of idolatry practiced in our past histories of religions that denied the *imago Dei.* Our lives in those situations were largely livid in the context of fear and unending struggles that broke the human spirit from generation to generation or two with unforgiving wars tribal and personal in nature. In some situations we continue to demonize one another, distrusting each other's loyalty to uphold peace and justice as vowed. From lessons learned from the latest pandemic-COVID-19, let us learn to continue to empower each other with hope and the necessary tools and resources to assist each other realistically with goodwill that revives the spirit of the *imago Dei.*

The continued concerns of the Tallberg Forum actually has been keenly interested to engage itself in worldwide health education to further all types of aid programs that genuinely enhance the quality of human life-- socially, medically, spiritually, financially, and scientifically with added emphasis on the environment. As stewards of our Creator-God are we truly willing to pursue and do what's necessary, if we are to change the world to live more harmoniously in fulfilling our destiny as divinely designed since the beginning of time? Unfortunately, our mission to date has been only partially fulfilled. How can we hope to change the world, if we are unwilling to transform ourselves, to live in peace as we increase the fruits of our Creator without harming one another to gain a larger share for ourselves? (I Corinthians 1:10-19)

"Human life matters greatly to our Creator!" remarked Swiss Catholic Theologian Hans Kung at Pittsburgh Theological Seminary's 200th anniversary in 1994. *He observed that it was impossible to have peace in the world, without having peace and dialogue among the religions of the world.* Serious issues dividing the world population presently are both theological and scientific in nature. Both sides of the human equation need to be confronted as related parts of the whole. We can't live in separate camps with divided values, while working for peace at the same time. Whatever our belief system might be, we need to work together to address the real factors at the roots of global poverty. Every nation's population or tribe that is still forced to drink unclean

water, face inadequate sanitation, and suffer from illiteracy needs to be confronted by humans who do care, whether they are believers or nonbelievers. We are all humans which ought to make a difference in our stewardship together, whatever our economic and spiritual philosophies of life might be.

More than 3 billion of the world's poor exist on less than $2 per day. In parts of Africa today, 70% of earnings are much lower. While the wealthier nations supply large amounts of relief, especially when starvation is present, such charity does not facilitate realistic development. A famous Chinese proverb many have heard in their travels clarifies the distinction between development and charity: "Give hungry persons a fish, and they will be hungry tomorrow. Teach persons how to fish and they will never be hungry again." Our future ethical task is also to teach the importance of sharing one's supply of fish, and thereby to avoid overeating in one community at the expense of others.

According to Professor Ackoff, we all need to deepen our understanding of true development. It is much more than the acquisition of wealth or an increase in the standard of living as is often assumed. Professor Ackoff explained at Tallberg, that one's standard of living is simply an index of growth, not complete development. Quality of life is far more encompassing; we need to appreciate the complex index of development. Development and growth are really not the same.

Development is essentially an ongoing process; it is primarily a means of increasing one's competence, an ability to satisfy human needs and the legitimate desires we require for well-being.

True development takes place in the context of learning. It is self-initiated and can't be done by another. This is why most faculty members enjoy teaching and learning, especially in lively exchanges with students in the classroom. One person cannot learn for another, neither can development be accomplished for others or imposed upon them. There are limitations in online learning that can't be ignored in our expanding use of computer technology, namely, to educate young people "in the far corners of our global society on the importance of data information to enhance their engagement in building tomorrow's society.

The founder of the Tallberg Forum, Mr. Bo Ekman, is a Swedish business executive and the son of a Lutheran pastor. He expressed in his opening remarks at Tallberg that the secret for being humanly interconnected is to *"walk the talk"* of our faith each day. He said, "When you listen to your own true voice, then you speak a universal language. We all share a dream, a beautiful dream, of common purpose for a better life. For ourselves and for generations to come, we seek a reverence for all life in our universe that includes planet earth." Ekman is referring to the spirit of the *imago Dei,* expressed in *Genesis 1: 26-27.* Ekman also quoted from Dag Hammarskjold's posthumous book *Markings*

(Alfred Knopf, New York): *"The more faithfully you listen to the voice within you, the better you will hear what is sounding outside. And only he (or she) who listens can speak"*.

The unending challenge is to interpret and integrate all the dimensions of our lives – physical, spiritual and intellectual, accepting the larger reality that every need of ours may not always be of equal value before God. Like the earlier disciples of Jesus, we need to confront those preconceived answers to our questions. Jesus often responded in silence or with another unexpected question. Jesus had keen on his understanding of human nature, having submitted himself to the *Will of God* rather than simply following his own voice in his process of discernment.

A wider vision can lead us to *common ground* which recognizes a shared stewardship under our Creator that encompasses the universe. It is this shared responsibility that deserves our mutual loyalty and *global citizenship under God. "In God We Trust"* will then be also our *global motto for citizenship that* adds meaning *to the unity of humankind.* This duality of outlook can inspire and encourage us towards peace and justice for all. With **Heaven's Passport for a fuller life on earth** that represents our values, we will enhance our group discussions in our travels, as we uncover a deeper understanding of *the common good* in our expanded conversations together.

The Library of Alexandria in Egypt has begun to issue *global library cards* with emphasis on medical education for those interested in its *Supercourse Program* started some years ago in cooperation with faculty colleagues at the University of Pittsburgh. Increasing such activity internationally ought to be strongly encouraged.

Scripture to consider:
Genesis 9:8-17 & Revelation 21 and 22
Proverbs 6:9-35
Mark 13:1-37
John 3:16
I Corinthians 1:10-19
1 John, 2 John & 3 John (God and love are inseparable)
Psalm 27, 41, & Isaiah 6:1-**13** (After an apocalypse a field of stumps accepts God's challenge to plant with special care seeds of renewal.)

Books and articles for classroom and neighborhood discussions:
Thomas E. Torrance, *The Apocalypse Today,* James Clarke & Co., UK

Eugene H. Peterson, *Reversed Thunder*: *The Revelation of John & the Praying Imagination*, Harper & Row, New York

Richard R. Hays, *The Moral Vision of the New Testament: A Contemporary Introduction to New Testament Ethics*, Harper, San Francisco

Jurgen Moltmann, *Theology of Hope,* SCM Press LTD, London

Environmentalists James Lovelock & John Seabrook, *"Sowing for Apocalypse: The Quest for a Global Seed Bank", The New Yorker, 8/27/07*

News of a Bavarian State Opera performed by the children of immigrants on the theme of Moses is reported by Joshua Barone in the *Arts Section* of *The New York Times,* August 13, 2018. The performance is understood as a young people's version of apocalypse in their lives.

Other stories told by Mimi Swartz, *"Talking Apocalypse with My Son",* January 16; and Andrew Schmiege, *"A Proust-Apocalyptic Story",* January 22; both articles in *The New York Times,* 2018

Alex Williams, *"Essentials for the Apocalypse",* New *York Times, September27, 2017*

Editorial, "The Coronavirus Crisis Inside Prisons", The New York Times, June *20, 2020*

L. Rafael Reif, *"We Need Foreign Students",* The New *York Times,* July 16, 2020. President Reif is at MIT.

Chapter 16. The Power of Weakness

Do you recall the last time you felt normally weak before the pandemic crisis began? Was it just before exams? Or was it due to a particular personnel issue confronting your research institute? Were you going to face tough decisions again? Perhaps your weakness was on the eve of your wedding with last minute doubts. Did you borrow too large a sum of money for your first home mortgage payment? I suspect some of us have had our weaker moments when being reprimanded. Others have had feelings of weakness under circumstances that were oppressive, overwhelming us with discomfort and dismay. No doubt we all feel weak when our self-esteem is questioned.

It is precisely in our times of weakness that we reach within ourselves asking for renewed power through prayer, seeking words of encouragement that enable us to complete our promised project. In some situations, we have all felt the need to have some private time with a trusted friend, a wise pastor or even a complete stranger to boost our spirits in the face of unwanted realities. Think of the Apostle Paul writing epistles to friends and followers during his journeys through the Greek Orient that led to his captivity. On a stormy sea, he was being blamed for the ship's poor conditions, he proclaimed unequivocally that even then, he found himself empowered in spite of his weaknesses, inspired by Jesus who had not forgotten him in his hour of need.

Jesus was calling Paul to be transformed from his past, and to participate in a new adventure as God's ambassador, which opened a dynamic new chapter of service fulfilling God's purposes throughout the Greek Orient. His earlier roadside Damascus encounter had turned Saul's life around. (Acts 9) The news concerning Saul's spiritual transformation and name change into Paul shocked many, and others were skeptical knowing his past history of protest against the ministry of Jesus. The followers of Jesus needed time to digest the transformation of Saul into Paul before they could accept him as the last apostle chosen by Jesus to serve in his new leadership role to fulfill God's direction for his life.

Paul used the story of his conversion experience to make a spiritual point to his growing congregations in Corinth and throughout the region with his letters (epistles) to an enlarged number of believers. Each having its special message to specific needs. No doubt Paul's story had unusual aspects and benefits for those who heard it, but one highlight rings clearly as Paul declares, *"I am content with weaknesses, insults, hardships, persecutions, and calamities for the sake of Jesus who inspires me, for whenever I am weak, then I am strong."* (II Corinthians 12:9-10) Uncovering the importance of weakness in Paul's ministry, I believe, was his most enduring and empowering characteristic as an apostolic ambassador of goodwill, in his travels throughout the Greek Orient providing hope as he encouraged believers and seekers to adopt the spirit of the *imago Dei.*

Paul's important means of learning and teaching was to travel to communities for fellowship—seeing new faces and renewing relationships with believers and seekers over a meal enabling us to become better acquainted. In our scriptures we have also read how Jesus invited the crowd to get acquainted, by providing meals after his lectures and then listened to their responses to his comments. These written and spoken means of communication from Jesus and Paul actually addresses our weaknesses evident in the remarks heard, but also witnessed in watching their eating habits while having fellowship together. Public and private schools now find it necessary to provide breakfast meals before classes start to assist students and teachers in learning more about each other. Kitchens and dining halls fulfill obvious needs in religious and educational institutions. Many organizations enhance their business/employee relationships with meals as well; this is also true within our armed services.

I had that experience years ago at the Pentagon. Have you ever seen the large Pentagon dining room reserved for officers? I was invited as a guest of the then Chief of Army Chaplains, Major General Kermit Johnson. We had been in seminary a year apart. Kermit was a graduate of West Point and had military service before coming to Princeton Theological Seminary. I looked around that vast well-decorated dining room, as we shared our different experiences over the years since seminary. I eyed the numerous military uniforms with gold stars, silver eagles and countless decorations indicating both rank and risks taken during times of war and peace. Here certainly was one measure of power. I wondered how that roomful of impressive officers would respond to a lecture (or sermon) that highlighted power through weakness? Could they really imagine power in the context of weakness sitting with members of the joint chief of staff reporting to the nation's president after Pearl Harbor or 9/11? Yet, haven't some of our greatest battles been fought in conditions where we were out-numbered and out-equipped by the enemy? Think of George Washington at Valley Forge. Recall the battlefields of Chickamauga during the Civil War, Chateau-Thierry in World War I, Wake Island in World War II, and Pusan in the Korean War, not to mention more current situations. Purpose and resolve can make Gideons out of those assigned to special-forces with their modest numbers and limited style of combat. Military dominance, of course, is measured in an assortment of ways, and does not exclude heroes who surface when caught in weaker positions. Stories of unexpected heroes are sometimes recognized years later when records reveal their exceptional service in saving the lives of others in battle.

Serving others in life is more complicated than many realize. In my teaching and leadership roles in Pittsburgh, I have had the opportunity to dialogue with the chief executive officers (CEOs) of major multinational corporations. They too can be unsung heroes in unexpected ways. The chief executive of a transnational organization is certainly a representative of power by most social and economic measurements. I remember well a conference of ethics professors as we listened to business speakers including Mr. Reginald Jones, chief executive officer of General Electric, best known in those days for its thousands of well-educated employees working throughout a world-wide complex of businesses. Mr. Jones was tall, stately and well dressed; he was well aware that he had a critical audience of ethics professors. He prepared well with knowledge of his vast enterprise, but also regarding the challenges facing the educators sitting before him. His very entrance into the room seemed like a touch of royalty. He was escorted by an entourage that included his pastor as well as his speech researcher and his own scholarly background. We felt that we were indeed in the presence of a knowledgeable corporate leader. I wondered at the time whether power through weakness would seem strange to Mr. Jones' ears.

As an active churchman, Mr. Jones might consider any admission of weakness as serving an appropriate role when participating in a Sunday liturgy. But weakness tends to be implicit in a seminarian's vocabulary along with humility, and may not be necessarily desired or welcomed in Mr. Jones' everyday work experience. He demands positive results from the many reports he receives regularly. He looks for signs of weakness, carefully evaluating the company's standing in the face of marketplace profits and productivity. Strong leadership was required as being paramount over signs of weakness. Such an analysis might be expected by investors and General Electric's Board of Directors. Most company leaders including our morning speaker might wonder if any good could come out of weakness, when confronted with bottom-line realities. Yet at the same time, I have heard other chief executives confess to me how powerless they have felt at times in the midst of their obvious power, when confronted with circumstances seemingly beyond their control, uncovering unethical practices that have tarnished the company's image. Sometimes they have experienced shocking betrayals from those counted upon to be loyal. Claiming inner power and seeking wisdom in those naked moments of weakness are the enduring marks of a strong leader that will be remembered and respected after the storm.

Some time ago, I took a class of seminarians to visit the White House. This was a class project on decision-making in public life in Washington D.C. As our White

House tour guide took us to the Oval Office, we sensed the tradition and power of the executive branch of governance. There is much power vested constitutionally in the office of the President of the United States even within the nation's check and balance system of governance. This factor becomes multiplied many times over when we realize that the United States is a superpower that has significant influence beyond our borders. There are knowledgeable sources currently that believe such influence is declining. Perhaps in the light of our coronavirus crisis our motto ought to be, *"Make America Immune Again"*. This theme was suggested by columnist Thomas L. Friedman of *The New York Times* for our reflection.

How would a conversation on the power of weakness sound within the Oval Office? Some recent presidents have testified to their feelings of weakness when under pressure. Lyndon Johnson was brought down by the consequences of the Vietnam War. Richard Nixon was forced out of office due to the Watergate break-in; Gerald Ford was judged for offering a presidential pardon to Nixon, and Jimmy Carter's influence was diminished with the hostage crisis in Iran and inflation at home. To our present day, presidents have had to ride the turbulence of political power as they confront limitations during their years of service in a democracy.

Additional articles are cited at the end of each chapter along with the book's appendix to keep our conversations current as we design our biblical

211

passports for a fuller life on earth. How interested would the Apostle Paul have been in designing his own biblical passport from his journeys through the Greek Orient of his day? Would it have helped him to face his weaknesses and restrictions awaiting him in prison in Rome? Would Paul's good news of power through weakness make much sense to power-oriented authorities and secure citizens of Athens gathered to hear Paul discerning comments on divine politics directed to their "unknown God" carry weight with his listeners? What about the gods of our day? How does our declared public allegiance and trust in God symbolized in our public mottos and pledge to our flag supported by our actions as citizens? Or are they simply words to support our morale and underline our freedom to worship efforts to boost our spirits and express our freedom of worship whether we attend or not. It helps us to feel safe. We might also hope as we design our biblical passport with the title "Heaven's Passport For a Fuller Life on Earth" might offer a sense of calm in our journeys with others that enriches our conversations and sharpens our observations on our trips at home ad abroad.

The challenges facing citizens who declare their loyalty to faith and country is that it needs clarity. For instance, why do Christians wear or carry a cross? Is it for their religious identity, keeping in mind the painful cross of Jesus? Seen or unseen the cross has two sides to bear in mind inherent in its design. One side states pain and crucifixion, the other side points to joy and resurrection. We may not think of the cross exactly in those terms when we wear or carry our crosses. The crucified side with its sign of suffering provides hope to countless members of humankind in their state of weakness, while the plain side of the cross celebrates hope and a future to every believer. For believers and others, both sides of the cross speak in unexpected ways to our common hopes for humanity. The spirit of *imago Dei reminds us of the importance to keep human life human to the glory of God.* (Genesis 1: 26--2: 2-4)

The primary purpose of a nation's motto is to lift the spirit of its citizens, guests and the morale of immigrants still adjusting and needing a boost. It also advances a sense of goodwill that furthers a feeling of peace and unity within the community. Some of us might actually sense weakness inside of us without repeating our national mottos and pledge to the nation's flag. If the truth is told, we do feel weak about a lot of things that we simply keep to ourselves until this recent pandemic crisis. Are Americans simply superior in every way to avoid admitting their shortcomings openly? If that were the case, why would we emphasize our need to trust in God? Have any of us ever trusted in God completely? Would our lives be better if we did? Have we realized yet that no nation can go solo in its reach for greatness? Our mottos are more than a slogan to unify citizens facing a pandemic can be scarier than a nuclear attack? Perhaps the underlying struggle within humankind is locating just where lies our ultimate trust and loyalty, that nurtures our sense of freedom and hope within us. In short, what endgame are we pursuing

today that offers meaning and purpose for us? How honest will we be in constructing a biblical passport that's committed to a fuller life in the most inclusive sense possible? Anything less spells trouble for humankind. *What prevents us now from trusting each other to become a trustworthy team of nations advancing peace, justice, and hope for the wellbeing of humankind?* Have we lost hope when we are in agreement with Henry Kissinger's world of ***realpolitik?*** Is poet Aja Monet's reflective response to Kissinger adequate? **"Radically loving each other is the only everything worth anything". What do you think?**
Scripture to consider:
Genesis 1:26-31; 2:15-25
Psalm 90, 95, 99-104 & 118
Proverbs 11 to 13; 21:30-31
Ecclesiastes 9:1-6; 7-12; 13-18
Isaiah 40:1-8; 25-31 As we reflect on Isaiah, why do we persist on complaining?
Acts 9:1-31 Paul's epistles were his means of teaching.
I Corinthians 2:1-5 & Chapter 13 *(Paul's well-known comments on love)*
II Corinthians 12:1-10
Romans chapter 6 is Paul's outline to a fuller life!
I Thessalonians 5:5-25
Books and articles for discussions:
Joshua Rothman, "The Enemy Next Door", The New Yorker, November 7, 2016. Rothman, asks a simple but often overlooked question, "Do good neighbors make good citizens?"

Walter Johnson, *"The Broken Heart of America: St Louis and the Violent History of the United States"*, Basic Books, New York

Peter W. Marty, editor/publisher, *"Letting go of white defensiveness"*, *The Christian Century, July 15, 2020*

Chris Hoke, *A Church for Every Prisoner*, *The Christian* Century, October 26, 2016. Pastor Hoke writes that an important part of their church's ministry is to write regularly to prison inmates at Tierra Nueva in Skagit Valley, Washington State.

An unpublished sermon, "Responding to a Call", preached by Pastor Michael D. Kirby who participated at the Presbyterian General Assembly in Saint Louis (June 2018). His sermon included an illustration from the Assembly. Delegates discovered they had power in the face of apparent weakness as outsiders meeting in Saint Louis near the city's prison known as the "jail house" where citizens unable to afford bail had to remain incarcerated until their long delayed court date (even on misdemeanor charges), creating hardships for their families. This news ignited the Assembly delegates to pass a motion for an offering, which allowed 36 of those in "the poor house" to go home and work again before their court appearance. Surprising power resides in our weakness as we renew ourselves through our sacred texts. News of the elders' action went beyond St Louis. The recently elected district attorney, Wesley Bell in nearby Ferguson announced on his first day in office the start of a wiser bail policy in his jurisdiction: ***pretrial release without bail***, for misdemeanors and selected felonies, unless the prosecutor thinks there is a threat to public safety. In short, Mr. Bell said, ***"I do not believe in prosecuting poverty;"*** as reported in his conversation with the weekly newspaper, *The St. Louis American.*

Farhad Manjoo, *"How to Fix America: Spend. Spend. Spend.", The New York Times*, July 23, 2020

Chapter 17. When Beliefs Become Cardboard Dreams

As we enter a post-pandemic era with hope, our concerns for health and security have heighten nationally and globally, as we seek to clarify our purpose in desiring a worthy future for ourselves and others We have doubts in these difficult times, seeking to overcome the serious loss of jobs and the many deaths from the coronavirus crisis. What will be a believable destiny for us? Our faith is bending in many directions, while some are engaging in unethical shortcuts, counting on rule changes in their favor. Are we undermining our own faith and future destiny with nearsighted pragmatism? Have we forsaken our favorite Bible text from our youth, John 3:16, "For God so loved the world that he gave his own son, that whosoever has faith in him will not perish, but have eternal life"?

Another text taking center stage in our lives is not from our Bibles, but heard and sung on our streets and gatherings based on a familiar theme, "Papier Mâché", that has been called "street scripture" sung with feeling by the talented African-American singer Dionne Warwick in her album, *"I'll Never Fall in Love Again"*.

Eighty people watching TV show
Paper people cardboard dreams
How unreal the whole thing seems

Ice cream cones and candy bars
Swings and things like bicycles and cars
There's a sale on happiness
You buy two and it costs less.

Read the papers, keep aware
While you are lounging in your leather chair
And if things do not look so good
Shake your head and knock on wood.

Chorus

Can we be living in a world made of papier mâché
So clean and so neat?
Anything that goes wrong can just be swept away –
Spray it with cologne and the whole world smells sweet.

The texts of John 3:16 "For God so loved the world" …and Warwick's "I'll never fall in love again" are actually opposite strategies that leave us with countless questions and unanswered doubts. What kind of backbone do we need to face the real world? Do we need a keener awareness of life's temptations and the consequences for many who now regret lost years in their lives? A papier mâché world of beliefs will fail us no matter how attractive they seem as we are lured into our cardboard dreams. At the end, we find ourselves marching in a sad parade made out of paper and paste, molded and shaped into a collapsible globe and a wasted life. Yet the haunting words of the chorus keep asking the question: *"Can we be living in a world made of papier-mâché so clean and neat? Anything that goes wrong can be just swept away. Spray it with cologne and the whole world smells sweet."* Many tourists travelling the world experience luxury hotels, clean, neat, and perfumed, while by-passing the needy sectors of today's global society. As thousands of overseas students arriving from abroad know so well, even America today is not as neat and hygienic as it could be. We didn't need a pandemic to inform us of that unnerving reality.

Life could be simpler if we lived in a world of papier mâché as depicted in ads and seen on our screens---- a world that can be easily switched off or thrown into trash bins as we accommodate our emotional needs of the moment. Many beliefs and hopes for tomorrow are constantly being traded for the latest items we can afford or pay for later. Items of temptation never cease to have their appeal.

At airports and ports of call, we usually encounter strangers with whom we can discuss issues of the day. While circumstances and needs may vary, we can distinguish to some extent between fakeness & authenticity in each other's remarks. We learn from experience and disappointments to be observant in our journeys. Everyone's search for happiness and fulfillment can be similar in many respects. The love and care of parents for their children in Bangkok is as endearing as the love my wife and I have for our children and their growing families. Every child in the world has an identity that reflects the uniqueness of God's love. Think of it! Our Creator-God cares for humankind individually and collectively within their cultural and tribal diversity. God loves the world with all its complexity beyond our psychic comprehension. It should be no surprise that our Creator-God wishes us to fulfill the spirit of the *imago Dei* within the diversity of humankind, discovering one another as soul-mates within the expanding love of God as we uncover the wonders of creation. This demands closer attention to our sacred texts to better understand their use and misuse in our lives. Divine love, grace and hope unite us with humility and wisdom, educating us to envision the true nature of peace and justice among us.

While on our first academic sabbatical abroad, our young family enjoyed their first and fourth grade elementary school experiences in Switzerland and Iran. We returned via Japan including a visit to the 1970 World Exposition in Osaka including discussions with Christian minorities representing Protestant, Catholic and Orthodox traditions which had co-sponsored an ecumenical pavilion featuring a large image of Jesus supporting our fragmented world on his shoulders. His figure epitomized the spirit of God's love and hope for the world as expressed in John 3:16.

To envision our universal needs on the shoulders of a cardboard papier-mâché image of Jesus stretches one's imagination. Actually, the Jesus displayed in Osaka was an insufficient marker illustrating the heavy burdens of humankind at that time. Unfortunately, these burdens today have become even greater.

Believers from all the major religions of the world today are in need of safety, security, health and meaningful jobs. Unfortunately, we operate to a large extent within a mentality that creates its own visible and invisible walls around each tradition seeking to satisfy specific spiritual interests. Each group tends to be occupied with its own community needs and interests without time or resources to assist the growing needs of migrants seen as strangers or "outsiders" threatening their welfare and way of life.

Migration is a dehumanizing and demoralizing process wherever it takes place, evoking a wide range of negative and compassionate attitudes. There are unexpected "saints" who show courage and concern to be helpful indicating that the spirit of the *imago Dei* is more widely spread than skeptics thought possible. There are also some caring & creative leaders among the world's religions joining forces to further goodwill. These forces of compassion are also embedded in the spirit of the *imago Dei*. Wandering and hungry migrants need most a reminder that our Creator-God has not forsaken them; they are part of God's family--and God looks to humankind to fulfill their vision to build a new life in the spirit of the *imago Dei*. Failing to act modestly and wisely betrays the good Samaritan in us.

We can begin by engaging seminarians, staff, faculties and laity of every faith tradition to organize as teams across borders to fulfill God's Will and purpose caring for one another as soul-mates. Unfortunately, religious voices today lack the united impact necessary to keep *human life human* as our Creator-God intended. We are trapped within our echo chambers refusing to hear diverse pleas for help, thereby missing opportunities to be "good Samaritans" as taught in our sacred texts. We need to surpass our silo mentalities and take risks to empower soul-mates with God's Spirit of goodwill.

We need to free ourselves from our towers of babble and open our doors of faith for God's Spirit to lead us to fresh pathways working as a team for the *common good of the imago Dei.* Adventures await those seeking to be faithful and creative, culturally and spiritually uncovering many opportunities starting with ourselves praying in silence and listening to the spiritual insights of others as we share the messages and identify heroes from our respective faiths to become a team of goodwill ambassadors for each other.

Our Creator-God is counting on us to fulfill the needs of humankind, working together as caring peacemakers *to do God's Will, realizing that we are called to be unexpected Samaritans in our diversity, expressing God's unique outreach that embraces us in the fullness and mystery of divine love visible on the mountain tops ahead.* The following poem by Bob Rowland is addressed to Christians, but in reality, it is a message to us all:

LISTEN FELLOW BELIEVERS

I was hungry
And you formed a humanities club
And discussed my hunger
Thank you.

I was imprisoned
And you crept off quietly
To your chapel in the cellar
And prayed for my release.

I was naked
And in your mind
You debated the morality
Of my appearance

I was sick
And you knelt and thanked God
For your health.

I was homeless
And you preached to me
Of the spiritual shelter
Of the love of God.

I was lonely
And you left me alone
To pray for me

You seem so holy
So close to God.
But I'm still very hungry,
And lonely,
And cold.
Thank You.

During a trip to India, our family stayed at the modest home of an Indian friend, a clinical psychologist whose patients came to his home-- Muslims, Hindus and Christians who he greeted daily at his door. There was obvious respect and hope on the faces of these patients. I had met our Indian host when I was a student at Princeton Seminary, and he was a graduate student at Princeton University completing his doctorate to be a psychologist. During his time at Princeton University, we seminarians were fortunate that he was assigned a bedroom and study at Brown Hall at the Seminary. Visiting India many years later, I was fulfilling a promise made to him that someday our family would visit him. In the evening we reminisced in his little counseling office, and I asked, "What is the secret of your healing power in relating to your people?" He replied quite simply, **"God loves the world, and so must we."**

As he spoke, my thoughts flashed to the previous day in Mumbai, where we saw families living in shacks, sleeping on the streets, and I wished that there were countless more dedicated ambassadors of goodwill like my host. Gandhi had rightly commented during his lifetime, *"even God does not dare to appear before a starving man except in the form of food."* In like manner, we can't say that God loves the world unless believers like us are willing to translate that love into fulfilling the concrete needs that can happen anytime.

I paused and examined my own thoughts. Any talk about love is lauded, safe, and expected conversation within one's spiritual community. However, do we really have any profound ideas of the real world? How many professors and students really know what's going on in the world beyond their studies and tight schedules? Unfortunately, we have far too few international students and faculty on our seminary campuses in North America. Increasing the number of international students and scholars would add greatly in understanding each other more fully. We need to be less preoccupied with papier mâché figures, cardboard dreams and video games. Let's be frank, within this internet world we are reading fewer critical books and articles to increase the depth of our global knowledge, stimulate our problem-solving capacity, and excite our imagination to explore unknown avenues to long standing issues. We have numbed our curiosity and lost the ability to express our thoughts clearly and creatively on our computers. While some of us continue to maintain private diaries, we are mostly engaged with insufficient diversity in our conversations. Since we now live in a tweeting global society, why not also stimulate group thinking across borders allowing young people and adults to further their growth in goodwill, by expanding creative relationships in our interconnected and interdependent world?

Perhaps we all need to step-down from our preaching pulpits filled with clichés and slogans. Perhaps we are trying too hard to stay safe behind our orthodoxy, afraid of heresy and even free speech. Actually, we have been losing courage to be relevant within our religious institutions, failing to explore fresh ways of connecting spiritually and creatively with strangers who might challenge the status quo. It seems the pandemic at least is stimulating change among us whether it has our approval or not. Our wake-up call is pushing us to learn more in new ways. We may be wasting time with travel if we spend too much time in the hotel lobby without making contact with strangers who might teach us something new. Have our fears driven us to be risk adverse? Being careful when traveling is important but being too conservative in this process may rob us of new adventures in a changing world. Travel can be more significant when viewed as an essential classroom of enrichment. It involves some preparatory study. A biblical passport can be an added support in preparing our attitude for encounters with strangers as we search for common values that lead to a fuller life within our global society, from our discussions together at our ports of call or unexpected discussions on the bus.

Today's learners can be tomorrow's leaders who can be relevant to the welfare of all. It is surprising how ignorant we remain when our traveling experiences are limited, or we are unprepared for our trips. First-time travelers may be similar to a prisoner released after a period of imprisonment, discovering that our global society has indeed changed in his or her absence. Morris West in his book *The Ambassador* (Bantam Books) captures something of our human dilemma in the following conversation between the ambassador and his wife: The ambassador speaks out in a rare moment of honest disclosure: "The similarities between our main streets and the main streets of Paris, Teheran or Madras are too close for comfort. I don't have very much respect for human nature, or myself either for that matter. Man's a half-civilized animal at best; so he needs a policeman to keep him decent on the street, and fellows like me to watch the aces up his sleeve when he plays international poker...Me? I'm a good watchdog because I don't have any illusions about anything. If your best friend isn't interested in the family silver, the odds are he has a yen for your wife. People are as honest as they can afford to be; and when it comes to sex, power-hunger and what they need for kicks, they're not honest at all. I'm an odd ball myself; so nothing

227

surprises me, nothing shocks me, and I'm always ready to hedge my bets. That makes me a good agent, if not exactly the man you'd like your daughter to marry!" "And do you trust yourself, Harry?" asks his wife. "Further than I'd trust anyone else, because I know myself better than most – even if I like myself less." "It's a bleak world, Mr. Ambassador."

The ambassador's world is not pretty, nor is it a world made of papier mâché. In the midst of such a harsh world, God loves us nevertheless and empowers us to be agents of divine love opposed to Main Street's bargain sales for cheap happiness. Every believer's response must be clear and unequivocal: happiness is not for sale, nor is it to be had cheaply. Happiness is found in being gracious--to forgive and to be forgiven-- with neighbors and enemies. Our world has turned into a jungle which we have been denying for too long. Now is the time to clear the jungle, to make room for common ground as soul-mates identifying each other's spiritual DNA, to understand and appreciate each person's strengths. Spiritual exercises like repeating a nation's mottos together can be a uniting factor among citizens who share a common understanding that such signs while not required of anyone, expresses concerns that our freedoms are being violated. Repeating *The Golden Rule* together can be another means of uniting us ethically as a global society. These public exercises of uniting us internationally as citizens can also assist us in developing our individual biblical passports to enhance humankind's collective citizenship for peacemaking based on shared values and goals.

Scripture to consider:
Psalm 103 & Proverbs Chapters 1, 2, 3 & 4
Proverbs 27:1-2 (This is a daily reminder for us not to boast about tomorrow)
Ecclesiastes Chapters 9, 10, 11 & 12
John 3:16 & Luke 6:17-49
Galatians 6:7-10 (God is not fooled: we reap whatever we sow.)

Books and articles for classroom and neighborhood discussions:
Robert E. Kelley, *The Power of Followership: How to Create Leaders People Want to Follow and Followers Who Can Lead Themselves*, Doubleday, New York

Michael Harrington, *The Other America: Poverty in the United States,* Macmillan Company, New York

Jeremy Carrette & Richard King, *Selling Spirituality; The Silent Takeover of Religion,* Routledge, London

Will Joyner's brief piece on Bill Moyers, *"Riding the Seesaw of Faith and Reason", Harvard Divinity Bulletin* Autumn, 2006. Moyers raised an interesting question to discuss: *"In a world where religion is poison to some and salvation to others, how do we live together?"*

Garry Wills, *"With God on His Side Throughout America's history, there has been one ally presidents have invoked above all others"*, *The New York Times Magazine* March 30, 2003.

Karl Menninger, M.D. *"Christians Belong in Jail"* on serious prison needs still neglected today, *Presbyterians Today,* February 1979

Peter Edelman, *The Poor Are Still with Us, The Christian Century,* Nov. 14, 2012

David Brooks, *"People Can Savage Social Norms, but Also Revive Them"*, *The New York Times*, April9. 2019

Charlie Campbell/ Dharamsala, India, *"TEST OF FAITH"*, *TIME*, March 18, 2019. The Dalai Lama (83) the world's leading Buddhist from Tibet is exiled in India.

Tara Isabella Burton, *"The Future Of Christianity Is Punk"*, *The New York Times,* Sunday 10, 2020, reports on *"Weird Christianity"* referring back to Christianity's historical past--ecumenical in spirit-- with an emphasis on seeking God's Will in our relationships, as we honor the spirit of the *imago Dei in caring for each other.*

Nicholas Kristof, "McDonald's Workers in Denmark Pity Us", The New York Times, May 10, 2020 is a timely report on Danish capitalism in a changing world.

Karen Strassler, "What We Lose When We Go from the Classroom to Zoom", The New York Times, May 10, 2020. Professor Strassler evaluates the importance of class lecturing with student dialogue.

Part VI: Speak Briefly, Act Wisely

Chapter 18. Business of Religion in a Market-Driven Society

A business friend that I have long observed attends his church's Saturday vesper service regularly as a preparatory time of confession before Sunday's worship service.

"Why are you so faithful in your attendance?" I asked
"It's because I have more to confess than most people," he replied.
"Why is that?" I asked.
"I'm a businessman; and in my business, the competition is fierce, ruthless at times. I have been forced to compromise myself in order to survive. I don't like it, but what else can I do? At the moment, I see no other choice."

While reflecting on that conversation, I realized that he was faced with something more than a question of business ethics. He was struggling to have an honest relationship between his business with his religious beliefs. How did he envision this relationship? Did his religion serve to soothe his guilt feelings? Was confession and admission sufficient, knowing the difference between right and wrong and yet unable to change the situation? Did he want God not only to forgive him, but to empathize with him? These are a sampling of the questions preoccupying my thoughts following our conversation.

This businessman sees himself as a believer who ought to be neither praised nor damned but understood. His faith has given him insight into himself and human nature in general. He considers himself a sinner in need of constant renewal. The interplay between business and religion is highlighted in the confessional process practiced in his life. We see this also happening in the dialogue with popular CBS television programs such as Blue Blood and Madam Secretary. These two series on television can be related to many busy lives and families confronting unending tensions. The man I spoke to finds himself linked to a troubling relationship between his spiritual and secular commitments. He has learned to accept unresolved demands of the interplay as his personal cross. He apparently prefers this route rather than to rationalize his shortcomings or soothe his guilt through various forms of psychological relief. He knows he is doing wrong at times, and without any excuses for himself, openly seeks divine forgiveness. Yet at the same time, he believes that he cannot conduct his business and personal interests otherwise if he wishes to survive, to feel fulfilled and to support his family.

Faced with this dilemma, what advice can we offer that is realistic? How can we help him to succeed at business and remain faithful to the standards of his faith? What other options are open to him? He refuses to divorce himself from the church.

Businesses are essentially profit-oriented; they are the means of livelihood for the entrepreneur, employer and employee. A successful business provides monies necessary to live, to enjoy good health, and to satisfy basic concerns. Ours is a business-oriented culture. Yet we need to remind ourselves that business isn't the *raison d'etre* of our lives, although it provides us livelihood and a link to our identity. Business provides the wherewithal to obtain the material goods of life and serves as an important link in shaping our goals and values in life. Religion, unlike business, points us primarily to what is ultimate in life. Our spiritual vision enables us to question the status quo operations of daily life. It leads us to the end goals for which we are striving, namely our aspirations, relationships and dreams that are divinely based. One's religious vision judges the very content of our living. It reveals our nakedness. It singles out what aims are short sighted and unworthy of our devotion. Goodwill ambassadors in business need to see the larger picture guiding us beyond the immediate pressures facing our neighbors and friends at the moment.

There is always the danger that business in addition to whatever else confronts us will become our (false) religion. When the means become the ends, we are in danger of losing self-respect, defacing the image of God *(the imago Dei)* in us and in others. Authentic religion warns us against this danger; it highlights the consequences of worshipping a "golden calf" that takes over our lives. My faithful friend was attempting to maintain an uncomfortable interplay between religion and business. Whether he will be able to sustain the interplay is another question. To avoid the effort opens wider the doors of idolatry, producing golden calves without love or forgiveness.

There have also been those who have turned their religion into a business, making the former a profitable commodity filled with false promises. Here the tensions between means and ends have been distorted and even destroyed. To prevent this, we need to separate the task of business and the purpose of religion. At all costs, we must avoid the temptation to baptize either into the image of the other. We need to lift up the essential integrity of each, if the relationship is to be vital and beneficial. Instinctively, this is what my friend sought as he confessed his errors weekly. He sought to overcome the temptation of cheap rationalizations and psychological excuses.

A good relationship between business and religion is one in which the separate visions and concepts of reality are recognized. No one can live a one-dimensional existence. The means of livelihood and the transcendent dimensions of life must be related. Preoccupied with only business, we come to regard the profit and loss column as the ultimate reality of our existence. How sterile our lives would then become! At the same time, an obsession with a spiritualized religion perverts our perspective and deafens us to the struggles facing colleagues and those nearing the poverty line. Religious reality informs us that identities and destinies are far more important than any immediate trade-offs that rob us of integrity and vision for a better tomorrow. A living faith will keep the cutting edge of that concern before us without compromise.

The biblical witness within our sacred texts reminds us that the primary goal of life is to give honor to our Creator-God in whose image we are all created. Honoring God implies honoring neighbors as well, since we are uniquely created in *the image of God* whether or not we admit it. There is no justifiable reason to dishonor either God or neighbor when we truthfully practice our faith. Since our standards are sacred, we find ourselves like my business friend, in need of confessing our shortcomings regularly.

The tough reality is that none of us can go through life before God and others without forgiving or being forgiven in our relationships. Unfortunately, we are at times working in an unforgiving environment that does more blaming than forgiving, as we recall the scars that have affected us so negatively. To forgive and be forgiven should be our desired transaction to enable genuine healing to happen.

When business is viewed as a means, it will inform us that short-term gains are not worth the price of losing self-respect or regard for others. Religion challenges us to widen our myopic perspective, to avoid the endless temptations that we would likely later regret. Problems take time to heal, if they heal at all. It requires our willingness to face the daily skirmishes and battles of the marketplace. Most issues need to be faced wisely and pay the necessary cost involved. Suffering between parties can be an inescapable hurdle that lasts for a lifetime and expands into a larger issue for the next generation to tackle in their lifetime. So far, it seems my business friend has not found peace as he faces his business problems. He feels numbed at times from the experience and unfaithful to God. Will he be willing then to carry his sense of defeat and wounded reputation to his grave? There are others, of course, who may simply sidetrack their problems, or find other "friends" to assist them, only to find that they have traded their soul in an imperfect world having nothing in return.

Another questions that confronts us in our travels through life, is how will we practice goodwill when the need is so great? Whose needs do we address first and what motivates us to do so? In short, how do we become effective ambassadors of goodwill through our businesses and foundations? How do we distribute wisdom and wealth in fulfilling God's Will in the spirit of the *imago Dei*? As we design our biblical passports, will we gain insight in answering these questions along

240

with our doubts? Will our biblical passports address honestly the diversity uncovered in our communities locally, nationally and globally? Will our data be complete?

There are always risks in the process of caring for one another, as we seek to honor God's image faithfully. The means and ends of our lives are inextricably related; means determine ends and ends determine means. Both need to be reviewed in the light of God's agenda, whose wisdom is more farsighted than ours to advance the community's future. Will we learn the lessons of applied ethics in the marketplace, building trust based on shared values?

The questionnaire below can assist us in exploring these marketplace questions as we discuss the usefulness of our biblical passports for future business partnerships.

MARKETPLACE ETHICS LOCALLY & GLOBALLY
Prepared by Dr. C.S. Calian

1. In your experience, has the chief executive set the ethical climate?

_____ completely _____considerably
_____minimally _____ not at all

2. How is the ethical climate in your organization upheld?

_____regulations _____trusting atmosphere
_____rewards and punishment
_____other

3. How do you regard your organization or business to be ethical? Because…

_____ product is beneficial for people
_____means of production considers well-being of employees _____production process does not endanger health
_____wages are good _____ all of these _____ other

4. Are most codes of ethics superficial or meaningful to a business organization? _____ mostly superficial _____ mostly meaningful _____ if other, explain

_____

5. Do you think that colleges and universities should offer a course devoted entirely to business ethics? _____ yes _____ no _____ ethics incorporated into existing courses

6. What do you think of Vince Lombardi's famous saying: "Winning isn't everything; it's the only thing!" _____ agree _____ agree to a large extent _____ agree slightly _____ disagree _____ uncertain

7. Has your company engaged in a recent event of ethical consequences of which you feel especially proud? Describe briefly:

8. When does salesmanship become bribery? _____ inexpensive items (rulers, letter openers, etc.) _____ moderate "gifts" (tickets to plays or ball games, lunches, bottle of Scotch) _____ expensive gifts (vacation trips, etc.) _____ other

9. How would you describe the process by which you make ethical decisions? Rank the following from 1 (most important) through to 6 (least important). _____ common-sense _____ self-interest

_____what the law specifies _____ company-interest

_____ religious principles (i.e., love, justice, forgiveness, etc.)

_____ other

10. Would you suffer a career setback or other subtle management retaliation if in a specific situation you put personal standards ahead of company expectations, and the management felt that business suffered somehow because of your stance?

_____ probably _____ no

11. If business is a game to be won or lost, should the ethics of business be seen in terms of right and wrong strategies and not in terms of absolute standards of justice, honesty, loyalty, etc.? _____ yes _____ no

12. Does an ethical posture improve or impede your company's business efficiency? _____ improve _____ impede _____ if other, explain

13. Does customer cheating make it difficult for you to maintain your own ethical posture? _____ completely _____ substantially _____ moderately _____ very little _____ not at all

14. Is it possible to agree on a common standard of values in a global society?

_____ completely impossible _____ highly probable _____ perhaps

245

_____ unlikely _____ impossible

15. Can you be honest, profitable and socially responsible at the same time in your business dealings? _____ yes _____ no Explain:

16. What is your view of human nature? Persons are: _____ basically good
_____ good most of the time _____ bad most of the time
_____ basically bad

17. Do you feel the present ethical consciousness of your business community is adequate? _____ yes _____ no If no, explain:

18. Do your religious beliefs have impact on the way you actually do business?
_____ entirely _____ to a high degree _____ slightly _____ not at all
_____ I do not regard myself as religious

19. Does your company support what it says about the importance of product quality and customer service? _____ yes (describe process)
_____ in a limited way _____ no

20. How do you understand the phrase "business is business"?
_____ anything goes _____ money talks _____ everyone has a price

_____don't expect generosity _____ other

Scripture to consider:
Epistle of James Chapters 1 to 5
Psalm: 90:9-17 & Psalm 140 (What is God's goodwill for the faithful?)
Proverbs: 3:5-6; Ecclesiastes 5
Luke 6:20-49; 10:25-37

Books to consider and a Reinhold Niebuhr film:

Reinhold Niebuhr, *Moral Man and Immoral Society: A Study in Ethics and Politics,* Charles Scribner's Sons, New York. There is also Martin Dobllmeier's film entitled, *"An American Conscience: On Reinhold Niebuhr's Life."* Niebuhr's social reflections began with his early pastoral ministry in Detroit, which gained increasing attention among clergy, businesses & factory workers of all cultures and ages. A brief sampling of his early observations can be found in his book, *Leaves from The Notebook of a Tamed Cynic,* W J K Press, Louisville

Alfred Balk, *The Religion Business,* W J K Press, Louisville

Kevin M. Kruse, *ONE NATION UNDER GOD: How Corporate America Invented Christian America,* Basic Books, New York. Dr. Kruse is at Princeton University.

Duff McDonald, *The Golden Passport: Harvard Business School, The Limits of Capitalism and the Moral Failure of the MBA Elite,* Harper Business, New York.

Articles plus a proposal for classroom and neighborhoods discussions:

Albert Einstein was known to repeat often the following statement: "ONCE YOU STOP LEARNING, YOU START DYING.", The New York Times, May 7, 2017. The late Professor Thomas Torrance, an internationally recognized theologian at the University of Edinburgh wrote *"GOD And EINSTEIN", Reflections, Spring, 1998, Center of Theological Inquiry* in Princeton, New Jersey.

A PROPOSAL: For communities & chapters of Rotary International wishing to initiate group discussions to design a personal passport on faith-oriented values for their travels at home and abroad, building mutual understanding and trust together.

The headquarters of Rotary International is located in *Evanston, Illinois* where we now live. I have been a past member of Rotary and appreciate its mission to unite leaders to support common interests in their communities building trust between citizens and their professions. Rotary members are expected to practice *Rotary's FOUR WAY TEST: "Of the things we think, say or do: (1) Is it the TRUTH? (2) Is it FAIR? (3) Will it build GOODWILL and BETTER FRIENDSHIPS? & (4) Will it be BENEFICIAL?"*

Pico Iyer, *"The Humanity We Can't Relinquish"*, *The New York Times,* August 12, 2018

David Brooks, *"The Moral Peril of Meritocracy"*, *The New York Times*, April 7, 2019. Brooks views life as climbing two mountains—the *first for happiness* and the *second for the transcendence of* self, based on his latest book, *The Second Mountain,* Random House, New York.

Adam Grant, *"An Apology Is Merely a Step Towards Becoming a Better Person"*, *The New York Times,* June 1, 2020. Practical suggestions as we face our post-pandemic era.

Chapter 19. "Ten Commandments" for Today

When examining *ethical citizenship* nationally and internationally, every country is as ethical as the last time they were tempted to cheat on their governmental standards for trading and services. Some citizens wishing to maintain dual standards of citizenship—upholding their loyalty to nation and faith have their challenges.

As a result, we often rationalize around these dual standards--political and religious—and attempt to advance both realms at the same time. There have been periods in history when leaders and followers have been compromised in upholding dual pledges satisfying neither themselves nor God. (Mark 8:36) We are confronted in this pandemic crisis of Covid-19 to focus more clearly on why separation in religious and state issues as expressed in First Amendment Establishment Clause matters. Dual loyalties inevitably lead to dilemmas for citizens as well as religious institutions with financial needs recognized in the present pandemic

Paycheck Protection Program. (See *"The Demise of the Wall Between Church and State", The New York Times,* June 9, 2020, by Nelson Tebbe, professor, at Cornell Law School, Micah Schwartzman and Richard Schragger both professors at the Virginia School of Law.)

To sort out a nation's ethical practices nationally and internationally is never easy. Much time is spent negotiating ethical trade-offs at the grassroots level and later expanded perhaps for worthy but questionable causes at home and abroad in conflict with the First Amendment Establishment Clause. I suspect deals in business and politics have always been difficult, especially for traders tempted with attractive opportunities having questionable consequences. Trading "upward" calls for refocusing perspectives and rationalizing that tempts us to dismiss principles we hold dear. The warning signs surface, but the rewards are tempting and violate our pledge to some degree nationally and religiously as we reflect on what's at stake. Our visions for a better life may be shortsighted and naïve or even selfish as we review past histories of wars and killings. The final judgment can be left to a panel of experts or with more humility perhaps as we pray to God for wisdom, seeking to bring to an end to our histories of unforgiving wars whether at home and abroad, looking for a strategy of peacemaking without further guns to live in peace honoring the spirit of the *imago Dei.* Or are we simply condemned to fruitless battles and gun-wars leaving an endless trail of broken promises protecting our self-interests, reducing our status as soul-mates, and sidestepping the *imago Dei* as well.

A telling example is the tormented life of Charles Van Doren, the well-educated NBC quiz-show champion of past years who deeply regretted his participation in a scandalous quiz program of that era. Read for yourself his story in *The New Yorker,* 2008, and more recent articles in *The New York Times* by Robert D. McFadden and Bret Stephens, Apr, 11-12, 2019. No doubt, we can all be sidetracked among the countless temptations that surround us. We too might also blame others for getting us involved in unsavory plots. In biblical language we might say we failed in fulfilling God's purpose due to our own nearsighted outlook and lack of trust in God and others to further our advancements in life.

A chapter on the "Ten Commandments for Today" is our means of questioning whether or not we have ever been in sync with God's Will. Perhaps we thought life would be freer and more adventuresome without God. Perhaps we also thought that God had given up on us as well. What is meant to pursue spiritual commandments in today's changing world which anticipates expanding space travel and added discoveries which provide other perspectives from our forebearers with contrasting fears and hopes from yesterday's world. In every age, God expects humankind to accept fresh challenges as ambassadors of goodwill seeking untried pathways to fulfill our stewardship to our Creator-God and to initiate new hymns honoring the *imago Dei* as we maintain our faithfulness to our Creator-God, furthering the divine purpose for our lives along the following guidelines:

First, accept those we encounter in life as persons who are more than a means to another's end. To manipulate anyone is to deface the image of God at the core of our uniqueness and authenticity as a human being. To justify our self-interests at the expense of others is wrong. It is simply demeaning of others who like us will become soul-mates to benefit humankind as we learn to live together in peace advancing responsibly the wonders of creation as the stewards of our Creator-God. Our joint task is to strengthen creation and ourselves to complete our mission with humility and grateful thanks to God. In case we are wondering, God will be nearer to us in illness and trauma for our comfort than we realize, but most likely distant from us in our idleness. These reflections, of course, are subject to further study and prayer. (II Thessalonians: 3:10-14)

Second, be generous; the benefits will exceed the cost in the long term. The propensity toward greed depersonalizes us; whereas generosity reconnects us with our humanity. Healthy relationships are strengthen through our generosity that fosters kindness among us. *Learning to love each other is the means of keeping human life human.*

Third, practice moderation; obsession with winning can lead to cheating and destruction. Some competition among us is inevitable; but why waste ourselves in seeking to win at any cost? The outcome is generally a lose-lose proposition for all sides of every issue. This is why rules and regulations are necessary teaching us to compete fairly, as we come to terms with our competitive nature, correcting our imperfect tendencies whatever the temptations.

Fourth, disclose mistakes. *Admitting error and restitution are necessary means to restoring moral character and true friendship.* Being ethical is never cheap but succumbing to our faults is harmful and costly as we review past and present relationships and personal histories.

Fifth, arrange priorities; have long-range goals and principles in mind. In the midst of marketplace trade-offs, learn to distinguish between primary and secondary priorities is an imperative. Priorities that honor life are always primary and non-negotiable.

Sixth, keep promises; enduring trust, confidence, and authenticity are built over a period of time. *There is no easy formula for developing trust; it needs to be earned daily.*

Seventh, tell the truth. Falsifying information destroys credibility. Lying is endemic to our lives; even etiquette fosters lying, destroying candor in relationships. Speaking the truth is not a science: it is an art fortified by caring concern for others whatever their perspective might be. *Lying is lying; let's not cheat ourselves from enjoying honest relations with God and others as well.*

Eighth, exercise a more inclusive sense of giving; charity begins locally, but the call for help extends far beyond our homes, neighborhoods, nationality—it is global in nature.

Ninth, insist on being well-informed; judging without adequate knowledge is fatal. We can't afford to be driven by rumor rather than facts. While having all the facts may be impossible, we must nevertheless maximize our knowledge as a prerequisite for wiser decisions. *Having facts is essential if we wish to develop trusting relationships in our interconnected lives.*

Tenth, be productive without losing your soul in the process; evaluate your life in light of your trade-offs. The meaning of success is much more than an accounting of dollars and material wealth. Nurture a life beyond work, work, and more work. Schedule yourself and colleagues as well as the entire family for a whole and healthy life physically, socially and spiritually.

Translating these "ten commandments" or guidelines into our lives and into our codes of ethics for organizations and company policies will support the health of our global marketplace as we evaluate our daily tradeoffs. We may be able only to approximate these "commandments," but in so doing, we will raise the level of business, show respect to others, experience personal growth, encourage efficiency, heighten listening and increase productivity. These are all characteristics for successful companies, nonprofit organizations, and respected nations if we wish to grow a sustainable and fulfilling future. Ambassadors of goodwill with their biblical passports in hand, will be at ease to promote a fuller life on earth, that enriches communities and nations in the midst of change, fulfilling our faithfulness to our Creator-God.

Scripture to consider:
Exodus 20;1-17; 18-26 (The Ten Commandments)
Deuteronomy 5:6-21 (A reaffirmation of God's covenant with Israel in Exodus)
Psalms 90 to 93
Proverbs 11 along with Chapters 22:1-29 & 23:1-30
Matthew 22:36-40
John 13:34-35
Acts 4:32-5: 16
II Corinthians 3:12-4:18
Leviticus Chapters 18-20 (Discuss Idan Dershowitz's research in *The New York Times,* July 22, 2018

For classrooms and neighborhood discussion:
Two films for interracial discussion are based on true stories: BLACKKKLANSMAN, by Spike Lee and JUST MERCY by Bryan Stevenson.

Frances FitzGerald, *The Evangelicals; The Struggle to Shape America,* Simon & Schuster, New York.

Randall Balmer, *Evangelism in America, Baylor University Press*

Aubrey Hodes, *Martin Buber: An Intimate Portrait,* The Viking Press and a more recent book from Yale University Press on *Martin Buber: A Life of Faith and Dissent* by Paul Mendes-Flohr, professor emeritus at University of Chicago, reviewed by Benjamin Balint under the title, "The Hebrew Humanist" for *The Wall Street Journal*, April 7, 2019. Buber died in 1965, a renowned philosopher & teacher.

Romesh Ratnesar, *"Philanthropy: A New Take On Giving", Time Magazine 12/2198*

Nicholas Kristof, *"10 Modest Steps to Cut Gun Violence", The New York Times,* May 24, 2018

Charlotte Graham-McLay, *"New Zealand Killings Spur Swift Passage of Gun Control Law", The New York Times*, April 11, 2019. Credit for this quick and realistic action goes to Prime Minister Jacinda Arden of New Zealand.

David Brooks, *"Neighborhoods Are the Unites Of Change", The New York Times*, September 19, 2019. Also, by Brooks, *"We Need National Service, Now",*

NYTimes, May 8, 2020. Both articles are timely as we recover from the pandemic-COVID-19.

Michael J. Sandel, *"The pandemic has scrambled how we value everyone's economic and social roles", The New York Times,* April 19, 2020. Professor Sandel of Harvard University writes a response to the pandemic theme being heard on television screens: "Are We All in This Together?" His forthcoming book will expand his concerns, *"The Tyranny of Merit: What's Become of the Common Good?"*

Chapter 20. Pakistan's Paradox: Facing Globalized Realities

Doris and I were looking forward to our trip to Pakistan to lecture at Gujranwala Theological Seminary. GTS was founded over a century ago by graduates from Pittsburgh Theological Seminary to educate future pastors and lay leaders for the modest Christian minority under two percent of Pakistan's population, which is predominantly Muslim. In addition to classroom teaching, we would be staying with a Seminary faculty family, and also be visiting and speaking in a number of churches, hospitals and related educational institutions largely supported by Presbyterians from the United States.

On the highway from Islamabad's airport to Gujranwala, we drove by the Faisal Mosque and a few weeks later had the opportunity to discover its significance in Islamabad and throughout Pakistan and beyond. The Faisal Mosque witnesses dramatically to the Islamic wave of revival and is regarded as one of the largest functioning mosques in the world. Its majestic simplicity is breathtaking. Architecturally it is shaped like a tent, reaching outwards to thousands upon thousands of devout pilgrims who enter its grounds. The Islamic University of Pakistan is attached to the Faisal Mosque which enhances its importance.

Our visit to the Faisal Mosque coincided with the weekend of Eid-Al Fitr, climaxing the end of Ramadan, a month long fast for Muslims during daylight hours. During Ramadan, believers renew their commitment of faith and submission to Allah's will, acknowledging and honoring the revelation of the Koran through the Prophet Mohammed, God's messenger. As I removed my shoes and entered the Mosque, my thoughts turned to the many conversations and concerns I heard during the previous two weeks among the Christian minority with whom we had open discussions and found ourselves warmly welcomed.

Doris and I kept wondering why the present renewal of Islam in Muslim countries had socially been at the expense of its non-Muslim minorities. Is it necessary for Islamization in Pakistan to deny the democratic process promised to all Pakistani citizens? During the election of 1993, Benazir Bhutto was serving as Prime Minister and leader of the Pakistani People's Party. She wished to further the constitutional democratic process of governance in Pakistan, fulfilling the wishes of the country's founding leaders in 1947, seeking to establish an independent Islamic voice for their country in the face of globalizing realities on the political horizon emerging then.

At that time, the principal founder of Pakistan, Mohamed Ali Jinnah emphasized equal rights of citizenship at the Constitutional Assembly (1947) of the new republic as he spoke to the delegates present: "You are free, you are free to go to your temples, you are free to go to your mosques or to any other places of worship in the State of Pakistan. You may belong to any religion, or caste or creed—that has nothing to do with the State." However, shortly after Jinnah's death in 1948, the National Assembly took steps away from being a democratic state based on Islamic principles of social justice. The State of Pakistan became the Islamic Republic of Pakistan which presently governs in accordance with the canon law of Islam known as the Shariah (the open way of its teachings) placed alongside Pakistan's Constitution and backed by a strong military presence. Saudi Arabia, Sudan and Iran are also Islamic republics governed by Shariah. The role of Shariah is absolutely necessary say the advocates of Islamic renewal. These proponents of the Shariah are grouped together by the media as "fundamentalists". Actually, the supporters of Shariah embraced a wide range of Islamic reformers after Bhutto left office, and years later, when returning to her country to enter public service again, she reclaimed her political leadership well aware of the growing opposition to her democratic stance. Unfortunately, she was assassinated while on a speaking tour in Pakistan on December 27, 2007.

The inclusive range of Muslims –from traditionalists to secularists to modernists and even fundamentalists—is not by any means all militant, calling for a jihad (holy war) whenever there is opposition, perceived or actual, to the fundamentals of the faith. However, an aggressive spirit implicit in Islam reflects its own missionary nature which also engenders suspicions of potential rivals for power within their circles. The zealous fervor among some followers' surfaces with a propensity for violence aimed toward Western oriented countries with influence and resources which many Islamists feel have undermined their Muslim culture and values.

The violence is directed not only toward non-Muslims, but even more so toward fellow Muslims, notably strife between Sunnis and Shiites. Some suspect that the mounting violence between Sunnis and Shiites is fueled by Iran (dominated by Shiites) and Saudi Arabia (dominated by Sunnis) in a battle for control of the Muslim world. There have been many public killings in Karachi and the surrounding areas. The assassination of two American diplomats in Pakistan and also the murder of *The Wall Street Journal* reporter Daniel Pearl in Karachi was shocking. These could be connected to a retaliatory attack for the capture of the terrorist suspect Ramzi Yousef in Islamabad, who allegedly was behind the World Trade Center bombing, and the trial of Sheik Omar Abdul Rahman in New York City.

Another case of public interest during our visit in Pakistan, was a charge against two Pakistani Christians who allegedly violated the Blasphemy Law (295-C) by desecrating the Koran. The charges were denied by the defendants and the Lahore High Court over-ruled a Lower Court decision which had sentenced the two Christians to death. The Lahore High Court considered the evidence against Salamat Masih (age 14) and Rahmat Masih (age 42) insufficient. Both were acquitted and charges were dropped. Following the public trail, both Salamat and Rahmat were secretly flown to Germany where they were given temporary political asylum prior to a longer-term sanctuary in Scandinavia.

The court case of Salamat and Rahma actually occurred not far from Gujranwala Seminary where we were staying at the faculty home of Professor Aslam Ziai and his family. There was much excitement when the school's principal announced that whatever the outcome of the trial, all members of the Seminary community must remain on campus for the following few days for their safety. This story highlights the duality of governance in Pakistan which can be exacerbated between official judicial process upheld by the State's constitution and Islamic law under Shariah.

A more recent case of a blasphemy conviction was overturned by Pakistan's Supreme Court involving Asia Bibi, a Christian farm worker with five children who had already spent eight years on death row. Asia was

265

finally acquitted of false charges and freed to leave the country which protects its citizens according to the nation's founding laws, *"irrespective of their social status or religious beliefs."* (Reported by Salman Masood, *"Pakistani Court Upholds'18 Blasphemy Acquittal"*, *The New York Times,* January 30, 2018.)

The above cases and their situations demonstrate *Pakistan's paradox* for its citizens, residents and visitors. The issues deepen with Pakistan's on-going border conflicts with India discussed by Asad Durrani and A.S. Dulat in their co-authored book, *The Spy Chronicles,* reported in *The New York Times* (May 30, 2018) under the title, *"Pakistani Army Balks Over Book from Ex-Spy Chiefs of Pakistan and India"*. Another issue is the country's woes over its growing trade deficit of $ 36 billion, while also serving as the key supply route for the U.S. forces these past years in the continuing conflicts in Afghanistan. Pakistan's unsteady status within and along its borders are causes for much concern

Facing such globalized realities enables us to realize that Pakistan's Paradox also reflects other forms of paradoxes, which collectively increase the pressures on the surrounding areas as they seek reliable partnerships to become religious soulmates whose motives for peace and justice are genuinely questioned in troubled times.

Many observers consider Islam to be the world's fastest-growing religion. This factor could be questioned. The Pew Research Center projects that between 2010 and 2050 the number of Muslims worldwide will soar. The Pew studies point out that during the next four decades, Christians will remain the largest religious group, but Islam will grow faster than any other major religion if current trends continue. In short by 2050, the number of Muslims will likely equal the number of Christians around the world. This information is from *The Future of World Religions: Population Growth Projections, 2010-2050, Pew Research Center.*

As to the growth of Muslims in America, their number may already out-number several of our mainline Christian denominations. One in five persons worldwide is presently a Muslim, numbering well over one billion globally. Four of the largest Islamic countries are outside of the Middle East: Indonesia, Pakistan, Nigeria and Bangladesh. This factor alone testifies dramatically to the missionary nature of Islam. Saudi Arabia is continuing to fund financially today's resurgence of Islam, not only in Asia and Africa but among Western societies as well. Islam is becoming the second largest religious grouping in the United States, displacing Jews. It is already second in France. Their number is also growing in England, among the Scandinavian countries and elsewhere in Europe due in part to the current displacement of several religious traditions throughout the greater Middle East as well as in parts of Africa and Asia.

In light of this Islamic resurgence, should we continue to foster modest efforts at Islamic-Christian dialogue? I would hope so; but it's unlikely that meaningful conversation can succeed amidst intimidation and displacement policies practiced today by some government agencies throughout the world. There is also serious doubt that the vision of moderate Muslims is fully accepted. The Grand Mufti of Egypt visited Pittsburgh Theological Seminary over two decades ago and encouraged interfaith conversations with Muslim and Christian leaders and their students. Today's interfaith dialogue is advancing slowly among several faith traditions through the World Council of Churches, the World Lutheran Federation, and various Catholic agencies, as well as with a number of college and university academic interfaith exchange programs. Whether these efforts will lead to wider public understanding of diverse faiths remains to be seen, especially when hindered by our cautious attitudes toward strangers who practice their faiths behind other walls and perhaps see themselves as unwelcome outsiders simply walking by their place of worship. We can hope that the situation will improve as we advance ecumenical and interfaith learning opportunities and projects led by enlightened teams of scholars and believers of goodwill seeking to enlarge and enrich their life experiences led by the *imago Dei embedded in us.*

Whether or not we are willing to admit it, we are failing ourselves without meaningful exchanges among diverse believers who may harbor fears of unknown apocalypses and are comforted to realize they are not alone. We are all in need of helpful fellowship in today's distrusting society that tends to be suspicious of strangers. These concerns will not disappear; serious and honest discussions with study are required to straighten and direct our pathways ahead as we look for future classmates and colleagues who might become our friends in the spirit of the *imago Dei,* as we seek a fuller life after the pandemic is officially over, with the idea of designing before our trip a biblical passport as a discussion guide with fellow travelers from diverse backgrounds, which of course is the idea of this book-- bringing us together again for reflection and discussion as we revise our biblical passport based on lessons learned & shared in our classrooms and neighborhoods.

I remember attending a conference at the Army War College in Carlisle, Pennsylvania. The purpose was to build goodwill among tax-paying citizens like myself, to be aware of the War College's mission to educate gifted military leaders to face global realities serving as peace warriors to protect citizens and further national interests when necessary. It was a good educational experience for me that expanded my naive views of international affairs. It also offered an opportunity for extensive conversations with rising military officers. I was impressed by their candid concern to be responsible and skilled officers, but above all their desire to become tomorrow's peacemakers and goodwill ambassadors in conflicted and distrusting situations. The purpose of our Army War College is well grounded in its mission.

As I was returning home, I wondered if it would be in the interest of every nation to establish a *Citizens International College* to promote peacemaking and justice in a conflicted world. Students would represent diverse backgrounds building their leadership skills to potentially address the ethical complexities involved *in building a just world at peace.* How realistic is it even for us to discuss this topic in an imperfect world with its wide diversity of self-interests not in sync with each other? Nevertheless, as witnessed in the United Nations, most of these nations of all sizes are still eager to be united. Even those nations whose ideals have been defaced with the *realpolitik of the day as* experienced regularly with its national representatives, that the United Nations has still been worthy of its peacemaking efforts symbolizing humankind's hunger & hope for peace.

Doris and I have had the good fortune to travel to many countries and territories which collectively has made an impact in guiding us to appreciate the complexity behind global leadership within the context of cultural diversity. *The urge to harmonize our differences is always a challenge worth exploring.* Believers and nonbelievers are moved to discuss and design their individualized biblical passports as they reveal their essential beliefs, values and curiosity often expressed through their questions. The Swiss theologian, Professor Hans Kung challenged us over a decade ago to move on in our lives and imagine God's grace in action. Here is a brief paraphrase of Professor Kung's observations for us to consider: *"**Peace among the nations of the world is not possible without peace among the religions of the world, and peace is impossible among the religions without dialogue.** Unfortunately, it appears we are not a single voice committed to uphold a common ethic for peace and justice that unites us (as yet)"*.

Globalized Realities that Require Attention Now:

There is no doubt that Islam has appeal among biblically oriented faiths. Islam is not unique in expecting total submission to Allah and obedience to follow the Divine Will. Jews and Christians as well as Muslims are committed to doing God's Will in the spirit of Abraham, following the biblical tradition in the spirit of the *imago Dei*. Every faith tradition rooted in God's grace and love seeks to be faithful in fulfilling *God's Will, not theirs*. No doubt we are all in need of support, accepting each other in our diversity as soul-mates continues to be a challenge in life's journey for humankind.

I suspect many have fallen short of fulfilling God's Will, having chosen our own way instead. We ask for divine mercy for those who use and misuse the sacred texts to advance their personal goals. Our sacred texts are essentially *the gateways for understanding God's Will & Way,* and are not to be used as gateways for our ends or gain. Our sacred books are to be studied prayerfully for wisdom to lead humankind in worship before our Creator-God *& to place our pride in* *perspective, lest we forget Whose we are, and to Whom we owe our loyalty. Such acknowledgement frees us to be genuine and empowered in the glory of God's love.*

Designing biblical passports requires a mindfulness of changing conditions--visible and invisible learning that there may be an elephant in the room taking space and preventing us by clouding our thoughts from proceeding forward wisely with humility. As we design **Heaven's Passport for a fuller life on earth,** we can envision God's challenge for our lives in the spirit of the *imago Dei.* Namely, to let *"God be God",* accepting divine guidance and wisdom as we untangle our feelings and selfish desires, & clarify real issues and needs in life. *Relationships built on trust matter to God's people who come across our pathways daily from their places in life with hopes and pressing needs, grateful for the goodwill experienced in guiding them on earth as citizens and stewards to complete their citizenship in heaven faithfully before God. (Philippians 3:20)*

Scripture to consider:
Psalm 62, 63, 102, 140:12-13 & 119 to 121
Ecclesiastes 11
John 3:16
Acts 10:30-40
Galatians 3:27-29

Materials for Study and Discussion:

Dale T. Irvin & Scott W. Sunquist, *History of The World Christian Movement, Volume I: Earliest Christianity to 1453 & Volume II: Modern Christianity from 1454 to 1800,* Orbis Books, Maryknoll, New York

Andre Bieler, *Calvin's Economic and Social Thought,* WCC Publications, World Council of Churches, Geneva, Switzerland

Oliver Sacks, *Gratitude,* Alfred A. Knopf, New York

Kenneth Cragg, *The Call of The Minaret,* Oxford University Press

Harold Bloom, *The American Religion: The Emergence of the Post-Christian Nation,* Simon Schuster, New York.

Alex Nicholls, *Entrepreneurship: New Models of Sustainable Social Change,* Oxford University Press, UK. Dr. Nicholls is a lecturer at the Skoll Centre, Said Business School, Oxford University.

John Lewis Geddis, *On Grand Strategy,* Penguin Books. Professor Geddis received the Pulitzer Prize for his biography of *George Kennan: An American Life.*

Jeff John Roberts, *"Globalization Bites Back",* *Fortune,* August 1, 2017

Maryann Cusimano Love, *"Religion and Foreign Policy"*, *The Christian Century,* May 15, 2013. The author is part of a working team at the U.S. Department of State on matters related to religion and foreign policy.

Lamin Sanneh, *"Global Christianity and the re-education of the West"*, *Christian Century,* July 19-26, 1995. Professor Sanneh will be long remembered at Yale University.

William H. Willimon, "Interfaith Marriage: A Reality Check", *Christian Century*, May 29, 2013.

David Galenson, *"Tortoises and Hares"*, remind us that races in life don't always go to the swift. Sometimes the slower approach produces a better outcome, *Social Entrepreneurship Postings,* Spring, 2007, Skoll Centre, Oxford, UK.

Jon Wright &Jason Byassee, *"Islamic Wisdom: What Christians Can Learn"*, *Christian Century*, May 15, 2007.

Ross Douthat, *"Fear of a Black Continent"*, *The New York Times,* October 2, 2018

Ameena Hussein from Colomba, Sri Lanka, *"Fighting for the Soul of Islam, The New York Times*, May 3, 2019. Why is there violent ideology among Muslims?

Paul Sullivan, *"Wealth Matters: Investing in a More Positive Image of Muslims", The New York Times*, May 25, 2019. Anas Osman founded the *Pillars Fund.*

Part VII: Don't Quit on God, Others, or Yourself

Chapter 21. Sanctified Ambition: What Is It?

Can we expect greatness from our children and grandchildren? No doubt parents, grandparents, and friends carry these thoughts as they attend graduation ceremonies to celebrate significant landmarks reached by loved ones anticipating new pathways in their lives. How certain can anyone's future opportunities be in today's rapidly changing post-pandemic world? Most recent graduates detest the question, "What's next?" Some are planning for additional education but worry about increasing debts. Are there realistic answers for these ambitious young people? As role models, what responsibilities do we have to our youth? This is where sanctified ambition might be helpful. What are we talking about?

Sanctified ambition expresses the goal to pursue God's Will throughout life wherever we are engaged in fulfilling our responsibilities, knowing often that we are surrounded by constant pressure demanding our energy and time. How do we stay faithful with all that is asked of us? We are all so busy that it is really difficult, if not impossible at times, to uphold the spirit of the *imago Dei.* Such busyness does not seem fair to us. At times it looks as if God has left us without sufficient support. It actually appears that being overworked leaves us no time to celebrate. How much of our ambition and involvement are drying up, leaving us feeling unsanctified, neither satisfying our needs nor fulfilling God's Will? This is a struggle for everyone with ambition and should be a topic to discuss along with our biblical passports. Has our workplace become too greedy with our time versus other aspects of our lives? Do we need to reset our schedules for a safer balance on all fronts? Research the material highlighted at the end of this chapter for further study and conversation. Rebuilding our spiritual platform for a more sanctified life with God's blessing and direction is necessary, as we outline our biblical passport for future journeys and undertakings.

Our primary hope is to be educated and wise stewards of God's wonders so evident throughout our universe as we study to comprehend the stars, black holes and much more. *("Peering Into Light's Graveyard: The First Image of a Black Hole", The New York Times,* April 11, 2019) Pursuing sanctified ambition is an unending call as we uncover the sacredness within God's creation, revealing beauty and power from the mountain tops to deep valleys leading to rivers, lakes and ocean shores not fully known to us yet. Our journey from day to day surfaces the diversity within creation has well as our oneness in God's image (the *imago Dei)* inviting us to become soul-mates sharing the divine abundance with thanksgiving and praise to our Creator-God, whose joy has lead us in a pathway of hope--envisioning a Dream Kingdom of peace, love, justice and goodwill in harmony with Divine Grace that takes our daily breathe away with every step of beauty unfolding before us.

This chapter began with a question: Do we expect greatness from our children, grandchildren and future generations to come by God's grace? The signs are all there it seems from our limited perspective. Will our understanding of greatness reflect and respect the divine dynamics of God's love and expectation with the necessary humility that builds divine as well as human teamwork to make a difference that matters to us and our Creator-God encouraging believers to pray in the spirit of the *imago Dei.*

Jill Lepore, Professor of American History at Harvard University addresses a similar question in her book, *These Truths: A History of the United States.* (W.W. Norton & Company) Her lengthy study highlights our nation's divided history in matters of political equality, natural rights, and the sovereignty of the people allowing *religious freedom, which includes every American citizen's right for self-dignity in pursuit of their understanding of sanctified ambition.*

Professor Lepore quotes Abraham Lincoln, *"We must disenthrall ourselves, and then we shall save our country."* This challenges an understanding of America's history without any false sense of being exceptional. Many viewpoints of our nation's history seen through the lens of religious faith actually encourages citizens to be ***more exceptional ethically*** since strong relationships are built with candor and trust with each other through mutual exchanges and shared opportunities. Her latest book, *This America: The Case for the Nation* (Liveright Publishing) is based on her essays in *Foreign Affairs* and *The New Yorker*, presenting a call for a purified patriotism for Americans with a caring outlook for citizens as well as immigrants. Lepore's emphasis is on a more inclusive development of citizens present and future to strengthen the nation.

Whatever the nature of our future journeys are, our motto, ***"In God We Trust"***, expects that we fulfill God's Will by living in the image of God., the *imago Dei*. (Genesis 1: 26-27) There will always be situations to dissuade us from fulfilling the Divine Will; there will also be many temptations to persuade us to distrust God's pathway. So, we find ourselves praying as the Psalmist often did, asking God before every challenge to strengthen us in facing the encounters ahead. *"Finish what you started in us, God. Your love is eternal--don't quit on me (us) now."* (Psalm 138: 8)

Will God quit on me first, asks the Psalmist? Or will we quit on God? Who will be the most loyal? Loyalty is a major factor in every human relationship and has caused underlying tensions through the ages in every

Divine/human relationship as we study our Bibles. Such questions no doubt will stir differences in our home life well as in Congress, the White House & The Supreme Court.

Sanctified ambition reminds us of the importance of not taking for granted that we are fulfilling God's Will, when personal ambitions intervene. Fellow believers with courage are indeed important in our discernment process. The need today is to acknowledge our serious errors, and not blame others for our poor decisions. Has there been too much pride and too little humility as we review with candor before God our decisions, which required honest review for the sake of our democracy? Sanctified ambition helps us get started with humility, guiding us to be relevant and realistic in learning from one another. Such a transparent process can transform and empower us to become ambassadors of goodwill in fulfilling our stewardship that honors God & bears in mind the following steps:

First, be honest as to what our end goals in life truly are. What role has your family and community played in determining your career and ambition? Honesty is often very uncomfortable.

Second, enlist caring counselors to measure competency before undertaking major tasks and responsibilities ahead.

Third, understand the results expected of us. Will this be a solo or team project? Has the dialogue been honest with all parties involved?

Fourth, aim for excellence in whatever you undertake or seek to achieve. Think seriously about the energy level required. Prepare yourself physically as well as spiritually before launching a new adventure.

Fifth, ultimately be faithful to our Creator-God, by example, not merely words, in expanding the common good for all.

Sixth, practice a welcoming spirit. The heart of sanctified ambition reaches out to strangers even if inconvenient and remembers to support others in times of crisis. Be generous, learn to understand the needs of others. Take on the spirit of the good Samaritan and be surprised as God's grace opens our eyes in unexpected ways in strange places.

To sum up, what are the contours of sanctified ambition that leads to greatness? I have a portrait of Jesus in my study at home painted by William Zdinak. Any artist wishing to paint Jesus requires imagination, since there is no genuine portrait of Jesus. The artist Zdinak has put together an unlikely example of sanctified ambition, a composition of many faces drawn within the artist's imagination of Jesus based on depictions of well-known contemporary figures who are "sanctified heroes" for the artist. Some persons included are Mahatma Gandhi, Jonas Salk, Martin Luther King, Jr., Alexander Graham Bell, Henry Luce, Pope Paul VI and others linked together into a portrait that depicts a patchwork likeness of Jesus for the artist. Another more recent effort to picture Jesus is described in Eric V, Copage's article in *The New York Times,* April 12, 2020, "Searching for a Jesus Who Looks Like Me".

The definition of greatness in the minds of Zdinak and Copage combines their collected heroes into an image of Jesus that is grander than those envisioned by any single artist. Collectively their depictions highlight the many forms of suffering that exist, clearly emphasizing that greatness comes at a heavy cost. The steps leading to greatness require sacrifice, discipline, and also death. Can we recognize such greatness from today's governmental leaders, scientists, educators, clergy, medical personnel, etc. whose values and services have our deep respect and grateful thanks?

Zdinak's Jesus is an artist's composition of greatness, and no doubt there are many other images to depict with their underlying philosophies and theologies of life. Each can be an example of sanctified ambition. From this framework of dedicated lives, we are able to encompass a range of commitments to our Creator-God. Ambition is a universal trait embedded in humankind. It is the driving force within us to achieve honor, fame, a satisfying career, power, wealth, rank, and status. I would also add humility as another asset to gain trust in dealing with strangers, clients and colleagues strengthening the spirit of the *imago Dei in us.*

Ambition also involves an individual's effort to keep going, with hope for a better society of lifelong learning to improve one's understanding under the pressures of change. Tiger Woods with his golf and personal problems--maintained hope, that led finally to his major victory at Augusta's National Golf Course. His countless lessons during these past eleven years concern much more than golf. In Paul's letter to the Galatians the Apostle draws our attention to his biblical values— seen as the *fruit of the Spirit—love, joy, peace, patience, kindness, generosity, faithfulness, gentleness and self-control.(Galatians 5:22-26)* Paul expects us to uphold these values of sanctified ambition in our everyday lives as we aspire to be ambassadors of goodwill in our journeys through life.

Scripture to consider:

Genesis 1:26-31
Proverbs 30:1-20 and 32-33 (viewing our lives when aging before God)
Ecclesiastes 3:17
Matthew 20:20-28; 25:14-30
Luke 6:27-36 & 10;25-37 (Texts on loving our neighbors as well as our enemies)
John 7:30 & Colossians 3:1-17
Ephesians 1:1-12 and 22-23 (finding life's fulfillment centered in Christ Jesus

Books to consider:

Ronald C. White, Jr, *The Eloquent President: A Portrait of Lincoln Through His Words,* Random House, New York. See Lincoln's words in chapter 6, *"God Wills This Contest: Meditation on The Divine Will"*, (dated September 3, 1862.) Lincoln is considered to have written thus shortly after receiving news of the disastrous results of the Second Battle of Bull Run. His memo was discovered after Lincoln's death by his young secretary John Hay.

Neil DeGrasse Tyson, *Astrophysics for People in a Hurry,* W. W. Norton & Company, New York, a handbook for lay readers to probe the known and unknown of the universe. See also Physicist Lawrence M. Krauss, *"Voyages of Discovery"*, *The New York Times*, September 5, 2017. Dr. Krauss is a theoretical physicist and Director of the Origins Project at Arizona State University. He suggests possible ways in which humanity's future and the cosmos are related.

Michael Lewis, *The Fifth Risk,* W.W. Norton & Company. Lewis focuses on essential government functions that are now under threat, asking *"Who's in Charge?"* See also Joe Klein's discussion of Lewis' volume in *The New York Book Review,* October 9, 2018.

Articles for classroom and neighborhood discussion:

David Leonhardt, *"The Storm That Humans Helped Cause", The New York Times,* August 29, 2017. Leonhardt advises "One way to prepare for the next Harvey is to combat climate change."

Julia Baird, *"Doubt as a Sign of Faith", The New York Times*, September 26, 2014. Baird is a television presenter with the Australian Broadcasting Corporation. She reminds us that religious people are allowed to question the presence of God.

David Brooks, *"In Praise of Equipoise", The New York Times,* September 1, 2017. Brooks raises the question, *"What do we seek in a leader, and would we qualify?"* Another related piece is *"The Strange Failure of the Educated Elite", The New York Times,* May 29, 2018. What challenges (pro or con) would we present to Brooks if he were invited to a town meeting in your community? A. Hathaway and Scott J. Shapiro, *"Outlawing War? It Actually Worked", The New York Times*, September 3, 2017, based on their recent book, *The Internationalists: How a Radical Plan to Outlaw War Remade the World*, Simon and Schuster. The co-writers are professors of law at Yale University.

G.K. Chesterton's closing reminder to us: "The Bible tells us to love our neighbors, and also to love our enemies: probably because generally they are the same people."

Thomas L. Friedman, *"Tiger Woods and the Game of Life"*, *The New York Times,* April 17, 2019

Jeffrey Kluger, *"The first picture of a black hole: The supermassive achievement"*, *TIME,* April 22, 2019

Chapter 22. When Believers Become Mature

Some time ago news reached us that a dear friend, a young pastor and the father of four children, was killed in a terrible automobile accident. A short time later, a letter from his widow arrived. Left with the responsibility of raising four children, she expressed how much she missed her husband. In spite of her heartfelt loss, she was thankful that he was able to touch as many lives as he did in his brief lifetime. She gave special thanks for the young people planning careers in the church and social agencies due to his ministry, confident that they would carry on where he had left off. In her tragedy, she found reasons to be genuinely thankful for the support given.

But honestly how can we ever "give thanks" in the midst of tragic circumstances? How have we responded to the unending immigrant issues dividing and displacing families today, overlooking the supportive value of their labor and talents to our economy? Other costly matters confronting us are wasted lives due to opioids and other drugs, unfortunate gun killings, and the tragic loss of family members and heroes from the Covid-19 crisis having such an impact not yet fully overcome in how we live today. There are still emerging dangers on the horizon to alarm us as we need to stay alert. The search to improve the quality and safety of life continues to be an endless task.

God hasn't called us to be pessimists or ostrich-like with heads buried in the sand, nor does he wish us to be giraffe-like optimists with heads extended in the clouds. God wants us to be realists with our feet planted firmly on the ground. Our Creator-God is gracious and caring according to our sacred texts. This is why God placed Jesus in our midst to awake us to our real conditions and providing a fresh pathway for humankind to follow with hope. In return our Creator-God expects our renewed commitment that reflects wisdom, kindness, and generosity. The crowds that heard Jesus marveled at his plain talk and concern for their true needs. His remarks were focused precisely on their situation as he traveled through the countryside encountering questions and tearful requests from those on the roadsides and towns he visited.

In my biblical understanding of faith, whether in matters of life or death, we gain confidence that our lives indeed belong to God, beckoning us to be faithful. God is wisely watching our back, even when we might feel otherwise. The Apostle Paul (known then as Saul) rejected Jesus at first, but later became aware of his divine power on that Damascus roadside. He was spiritually awakened from his blindness and found himself guided to a more promising pathway for living. A new chapter of God's unfolding grace directed him in unexpected ways toward renewed life. Paul in turn now desired to lift the spirit of his listeners, leading them to a fuller and more meaningful life. It is in this spirit that he wrote his epistles and led discussions in his travels throughout the Greek Orient of his day. He appealed to an increase number of believers with his own series of commands and admonitions, *"Rejoice always, pray constantly, give thanks in all circumstances; for this is the will of God as witnessed in the life of Jesus uplifting lives with mercy and hope."* (I Thessalonians 5:16-18)

To "give thanks in all circumstances" is actually a command to believers, not to be taken lightly. It is also important to note that Paul's epistle written in everyday Greek, uses the preposition *"in"* instead of *"for"* as we examine our sacred text. Paul is not asking us to give thanks **for** every circumstance, but instead **in** every circumstance. Even with this propositional distinction in mind, this particular exhortation still seems to be expecting us to do the impossible. As we reflect upon it now, probably racing through our minds are personal events and items for which we are not thankful, but instead bitterly disappointed and dismayed. No soothing or clever manipulation of words is going to make us feel any different. How then, can we give thanks in every circumstance, especially those events that are so tragic in nature? As we design and discuss the contents of *Heaven's Passport for a fuller life*, we need to bear in mind the totality of possibilities that might take place in our universe, knowing that much of what happens in human history is far beyond our expectations and knowledge necessary for proper research, for instance, as in the history of pandemics and needed vaccines creating conditions that have reshaped the destiny of nations and humiliated its leaders & scared its citizens.

To be realistic, believers also need to confront their own unanswered questions with raised anxieties about possible harm that can come from unpredictable events in the future. Advanced warnings may or may not be possible. To be totally unprepared is a reality we might not wish to bring upon ourselves due to insufficient knowledge and inadequate research hoping to get by. An apocalyptic vision of facing a possible black hole can also signal a self-made sense of our own forsakenness, challenging us to navigate elsewhere in the heavens or on the seas, in the hopes of discovering an escape route in our ignorance could be disappointing.

In these moments of possible loneliness, we may realize actually that we have too few, if any, soul-mates, who are aware of the *imago Dei* and its role encouraging us to care for each other whether there is or isn't an apocalyptic force or other unexpected conditions to worry us. Are we prepared sufficiently and empowered by God's grace to respond to the unexpected in our expanding universe of planets and climate conditions?

Nations should address these types of question collectively rather than conduct painful and unwise political and economic wars and other conflicts that make no sense in a changing universe of realities. How wise are we (or any nation) about space in our current national policies and priorities? When the *S.O.S.* alarm is heard, how will we respond--*selfishly or on behalf of each other for the common good?* Has America and other countries forgotten the support they received from each other during life threatening conditions that are sometimes side-stepped in one's prideful ignorance *Why not require a lifetime course for all voters on the ethical values of international interdependence and its benefits for humankind?* Invite the United Nations and our education policy makers from 50 states and territories to be involved in the course development. How do we presently respond to a crisis or national concern today?

Some choose to react *philosophically* in such situations, acknowledging that we live in an imperfect world and perhaps an imperfect universe as well. We need to accept situations as they are, working quickly to aid those nearest to us, and taking steps for our own safety as well. God's presence may seem absent in our fearful moments. Philosophically we may confess our limits in helping others, but earlier in life pledged otherwise. Whatever the case, none of us claims to be perfect, as we rely hopefully on each other's forgiving love, which unfortunately is also not plentiful. However, in special times of despair, we have also seen a diverse gathering

295

of citizens and noncitizens unite in surprising ways as soul-mates, overcoming resistance to do so earlier.

After the 9/11 New York Bombing, Pittsburgh Seminary held public events with participants from New York City bombing sharing different aspects of that tragic event. Some in the audience had roots in the Middle East and were now American citizens fearing suspicion and ignorance regarding themselves about their homelands. This series in the Seminary's program brought together diverse institutions and traditions for a practical interfaith centered discussion which also questioned the use and misuse of their religious traditions in such controversies. With high anxiety and personal interest, these public sessions were well attended, sponsored by the Seminary's *Center on Business, Religion and Public Life.*

Blaming God is a theological stance sometimes taken by those who assume that the fault-line behind such tragic events rests on God's shoulders, who influences faith driven believers to ignite such tragic events. Conclusions drawn are confusing doing an injustice at times to particpants as wellas one's understanding of God. Any discussion on this topic must be more composite—inviting various sacred texts to be at the center of the discussion, also encompassing historic, political, economic, cultural, and psychological biases brought by all interested parties. Discussions of this nature must also have candor with one another. More comparative study of various beliefs (see appendix of this book for suggestions) is necessary in today's rapidly changing world filled with disbelief and distrust.

There is no doubt that every humanly engineered apocalypse in a nuclear age can destroy lives as well as the environment. Today's practice of blaming each does not prevent these tragic disasters. It builds instead ill will among us leaving problems unresolved. This places us in the crossfire of angry behavior, that alienates us from having a more meaningful exchange as we bring our feelings to the table for discussion with our incomplete data and insufficient understanding of the *imago Dei* embedded in our faith traditions and in some cases supported by our nonfaith convictions as well. Without preparing ourselves in the right spirit to attend such events is unfortunate and unhelpful in making progress to resolve conflicts that calls for fresh openings of goodwill in an era of human displacement and broken families. It might be wiser to ask ourselves how free are we in our fixed communities to explore a deeper understanding of each other's religious and political explanations to overcome our killings and open wounds harming lives and distancing ourselves from the peace and justice God desires for us all. God did not create us to be destructive, but rather to have *Heaven's Passport for a fuller life on earth-- **to keep human life human as God intended since creation.***

Why are we then in such a mess humanly seeing ourselves as failed creatures throughout our changing world? Why do bad things happen, or for that matter, why do "good people" do bad things? Have we forgotten that being ethical has many facets in our diversity as we attend the courthouse for our trails seeking hopefully to find justice in our constitutional decision-making process for an enduring democracy. We are presently in the midst of reviewing the practice of our democracy in the midst of added pressure from our pandemic crisis and its future aftermath still ahead of us to test our remaining strength.

Sharping our ethical awareness can be useful in our imperfect (reality-denying) society, whatever our social status might be. Until this factor is addressed fully, we will continue to follow those old-fashioned clichés repeated from our youth--"that's the way the ball bounces", or "that's the way the cookie crumbles", believing that this is what we can expect in spite of what the rules and regulations might be. During my doctoral studies abroad, I met a German attorney attending his Lutheran Church; who recognized my American accent. Hans had recently broken his engagement with his fiancé. In despair, he shared his suspicion that perhaps his future held no marriage or his strong wish for a family. Philosophically, he muttered in German that this was his *Schicksal* (destiny). As Doris and I were packing for our return to the United States a few years later, he came to our apartment in Basel, Switzerland to say good-bye. During this intervening period, he had fallen in love again, married and was now the proud father of a 4-month-old boy. At our parting, he mentioned that God had used our friendship to point out his need to give thanks in every circumstance. He felt that God was quietly working in his life even at his lowest ebb, in the midst of his despair and bitterness.

Unknown numbers of us may feel that way today in our pandemic gloom, reacting neither philosophically nor theologically, but in a spirit of bitterness. Some may even be shouting inwardly that there is no God! Life may seem like a ship at sea without a captain, anchor, or compass, bobbing on the waters for so many days until it finally vanishes beyond the horizon. If there is no purpose to our living, then life is simply one great abyss. Contemporary thinkers tell us that we must face up to this emptiness and realize that after so many years of life, our destiny could simply end in a pit of nothingness as we approach an unseen black hole or another pandemic or climate crisis.

I recall vividly a conversation in Basel, Switzerland with a young medical doctor who encouraged me to join him in a visit to the children's ward at the city hospital. "There you will see," he said, "children deformed either from birth or from accident, wasting away like vegetables. I dare you to tell me, after seeing these children, to offer thanks in every circumstance!" What response might we give to this caring doctor with his sad but experienced outlook? How should we respond as caring believers, knowing that this doctor is not looking simply from some intellectual, abstract answer, but a response that will relate to his compassion and the cry of his broken heart? Perhaps we too need to face life like this doctor, and not run from the unfortunate realities that surround us.

At that moment in my conversation, I recalled the memorable words from the famous scientific genius Blaise Pascal, who said, *"The heart has its reasons, which reason does not know."* (Pascal's *Pensees* 277) The most I could do at the time was to point the doctor's attention to a young family with three children living in that same city where he practiced. The oldest of the three children is their daughter Mary. She suffers as a spastic; Mary could neither walk nor talk. When you were invited into their home and saw her crawling on the living-room floor, it was a pathetic sight. You felt sad for her and for the entire family. Yet, after a few moments of conversation in their home, one could sense an atmosphere entirely different from what that doctor might have expected. There was love and acceptance and true joy here. Mary was indeed loved by her family, and she, in turn, loved her parents and her brothers. There was reason to give thanks and to know that God was working out some good purpose in their lives.

Yet for some, our reactions will be neither philosophical nor bitter, but simply a reaction met with silence. When tragedy or disappointment occurs, the reaction often is one of ignorance and fear, the result being that individuals wrap themselves in a self-made cocoon of fear and ignorance withdrawing to their inner selves.

I was surprised and disappointed to learn that the delightful country of Switzerland has a number of citizens who have taken this kind of reaction to life, slipping away into oblivion in sanatoriums and hospitals. The Swiss are not alone in this practice. Or take the incident in the story of a devout son who turned to alcohol following his father's death. Drinking a little at first, and then gradually more in the silence of his bedroom, he found it impossible to accept the fact of his father's death. (from Edwin O'Conner, *The Edge of Sadness*, Little Brown)

There is a fourth reaction which Paul commanded us to follow: *React graciously.* A philosophical reaction leads to frustration. Bitterness pulls us downward into despair, and silence denies the human desire to communicate. However, graciousness can supply a new attitude in our encounters with the riddles of life. Graciousness is by far the most difficult of the reactions mentioned by the Apostle Paul to the Thessalonians: To put it positively, the test of anyone's identity and maturity is in direct proportion to one's capacity to give thanks in every circumstance. (I Thessalonians 5:18) It is precisely at this point that we might consider how mature we are in our faith and convictions as we design a biblically oriented passport that can be helpful before life's realities. The question of our maturity matters in in facing the realities of life and the many unanswered questions that will confront us in our discussions together whatever our backgrounds might be. How will we react to Paul's challenge to us all—Can we give thanks in every circumstance"? No doubt there are those among us of all beliefs who have already discovered that it is not always greener on the other side of the mountain and valley burden with its troubles.

Volunteering as one of the ship's chaplain on many cruises, I have often wondered about the burdens the ship's captain might be carrying, as well as his officers, crew and their families during their long periods of separation at sea. This was also a similar experience for the Apostle Paul in his journeys. His epistles (letters) shared his health issues and the terrible pain he confronted.

Are you aware of Paul's story concerning the thorn in his flesh? (II Corinthians: 12:7) Paul thought he could be far more effective for God's purposes without such a crippling burden, but soon learned that only with his handicap was he truly effective. How many of us would believe that any effectiveness we have is related to the particular thorn or illness that we bear today? Actually, it could be our own burdens that others might be aware of that lifts their spirits seeing us in action.

It is strange how God works. Our attempts to decipher the *Divine Will* may never satisfy us entirely, but by giving thanks in our circumstances we begin to accept the reality of the situation before us, and slowly uncover God's mercy in our midst. This may be the way to confront, but not understand fully, the conditions that disrupt our lives as well as to enable us to uncover a deeper level of stewardship to our Creator-God that has surfaced from **Heaven's Passport for a fuller life on earth** expanding our understanding of the *imago Dei*.

Scripture to consider:
Job 37 & 38 Job finds no wisdom without knowledge
Psalm 40 & 139:23-24 Understanding the *imago Dei*.
Matthew 11: 25-30 Helping the weary & their burdens
I Thessalonians 5:12-21
II Corinthian 12:1-21
Galatians 5:1-26

Books, an article and a film for classroom and neighborhood discussions:
Diana Athill, *Somewhere Towards the End, W.W. Norton & Company, New York.* These insightful comments on aging are very much worth reading as you discuss your purpose for designing a biblical passport.

Randy Pausch, *The Last Lecture,* Hyperion, New York is helpful for all ages on matters of maturity and creativity that can enrich lives. This lecture was addressed to the student body at Carnegie Mellon University shortly before he died at a young age from cancer, He influenced countless lives as a goodwill ambassador on and off campus.

Tayari Jones, *"What Mandela Lost", The New York Times,* July 8, 2018. Professor Jones of Emory University presents these unpublished letters written by Nelson Mandela from prison to family members. The article highlights the high price Mandela paid for his many years in prison separated from family. Professor Jones viewed his imprisonment as the ultimate sign of state power.

Gary Krist, *The Mirage Factory: Illusion, Imagination, And the Invention of Los Angeles*, Crown, New York. This unusual book features three lives in the shaping of modern Los Angeles—William Mulholland, an immigrant ditch digger who became a self-taught engineer; D.W. Griffith who developed LA's signature movie industry; & Aimee Semple McPherson, a charismatic evangelist who pin-pointed the city's identity as a center for nurturing spiritual maturity.

Vanessa Siddle Walker, *The Lost Education of Horace Tate, 1922-2002*, New Press. Walker highlights the significant role of education in building maturity in the lives of young African Americans and the leadership efforts of Horace Tate, the first black educator to earn his doctorate from the University of Kentucky.

Jennifer L. Eberhardt, *Uncovering the Hidden Prejudice That Shapes What We See, Think, and Do,* Viking. Dr. Eberhardt is a psychologist on the faculty of Stanford University.

Joshua Rothman, *"SAME DIFFERENCE: What the idea of equality can do for us, and what it can't."*, *The New Yorker*, January 13, 2020

A documentary film produced by Professor Henry Louis Gates of Harvard University and shown on PBS entitled, *"'And Still I Rise', Black Americans Since Martin Luther King",* can be obtained from wttw.com or 773-588-1111.

Chapter 23. Faithfulness Through Death

Human death is inevitable. I was reminded of this at my brother-in-law's memorial service. Edward will be missed by his family, medical colleagues, and grateful patients who benefitted from his care and surgical skills.

How well will we be remembered? Have we given serious thought to our own death? Our relationship to God is also evident in our attitudes and approaches to death. I recently joined a large ecumenical gathering at worship to remember the pastoral leadership of Cardinal Joseph Bernardin of Chicago, whose life of service was celebrated not only by fellow Catholics, but also by the faithful of other traditions who respected his vision and pastoral outreach throughout the city. The Cardinal envisioned life as an earthly pilgrimage of gratitude to God, an opportunity to serve humankind in endless ways. He was often disappointed by the insufficient number of persons willing to join him in worthy causes. Knowing that his earthly pilgrimage was coming to an end due to cancer, he was at peace and grateful for the divinely given talents of others he encountered, and he kept to himself his own unanswered questions known to God alone. Was his death a good death for those of us who attended that service? Perhaps most might find comfort in the fact that he died peacefully while asleep as a faithful servant of God.

With the recent coronavirus pandemic, many deaths took place in a state of isolation and fear that often accompanies loneliness. Unable even to express thanks in their dying state, caregivers providing aid to the serious sick had indeed endangered their own lives; their actions enabled many of us to see them as heroes, allowing us all to speak more freely about death today and how we might wish to die. Such discussions will continue to increase until a vaccine is perfected, and fears subside. It seems unfortunate that the subject of fear itself has become a political weapon in a way on virus matters, but also toward other distant policy decisions in relation to displaced persons living here and abroad in today's global society as the poor condition of migrants grows causing violence, abuse and death in many locations. All of this has widened our worldwide discussions on death and the worth of human lives.

As we discuss & design our biblical passport, we will encounter many cross-cultural situations that exist in communities now requiring better health care and more just and humane living conditions for young and old. We may need more teachers as translators to help us interpret how various cultures weave their realities of dying within their culture and faith traditions, but even that process has become more complex with the spread of the coronavirus crisis widely around the world the burial of loved ones needs to assure the health safety of workers involved as well as those attending the worship service including clergy participating who are asked honor the faith histories of families represented in the burial service held at outdoor cemeteries. Reporter Alissa J. Rubin of *The New York Times* recently writes, *"A Cemetery for All Faiths, and a Single Cause of Death"*, (7/19/20) about a newly established cemetery outside Najaf, Iraq especially for coronavirus victims and the difficulties families and clergy face to faithfully fulfill their promises to dead loved ones. *The New Valley of Peace* cemetery was prepared four months ago in the dessert and now has more than 3,200 graves. The changes now happening in Iraq and elsewhere offer, I believe, profound changes in attitudes for believers drawing closer across faith lines in need of grave sites and services in spite of past struggles with their sacred texts, but still *honoring their faithfulness to one God and the abiding spirit of the Imago Dei, embedded in humankind since creation from our sacred texts.* Such events as *The New Valley of Peace anointed graves for persons of more than a single faith tradition, it seems we may be* building a meaningful bridge across faith traditions, with recognized histories familiar to some degree and hopefully helpful as believers showing our mutual respect for our Creator-God as soul-mates and fellow worshippers for the sake and welfare of humankind, now starting again by God's grace and love through the dying power of loved ones uniting us in the sacred desert west of Najaf, Iraq with our mixture of cultures and mixed histories of struggles with periods of goodwill for the common good. May the latter increase as we travel together with *Heaven's Passport for a fuller life to God's glory from now to eternity.*

In Sun City, Arizona, a community designed for retired citizens, where the reality of death and eternity is discussed openly by its residents. I visited a lovely memorial garden on the grounds of Faith Presbyterian Church in Sun City, where a common burial area in the church garden is reserved for the ashes of its members. These ashes are commingled; the church maintains a careful record of each member buried there. This common burial place in the church's memorial garden highlights the congregation's belief in the communion of saints. These believers in Sun City are realists; they recognize that we are born naked and will depart naked. A biblically oriented funeral service among these believers says it all – *"from dust to dust and ashes to ashes in the sure and certain hope of the resurrection to eternal life through Jesus Christ our Lord."* From Irvine, California to Sun City, Arizona where might we place our own thoughts and feelings presently? How will each of us deal with death? Whatever we think, life's realities are not all neatly spelled out.

In the memories of many Pittsburgh citizens resides the terrible loss of 132 persons in the fatal U.S. Air Flight 427 over Hopewell Township, Pennsylvania on

September 11, 2001. Alive one moment and gone the next. It is difficult to believe even now; it is more than the human psyche can bear at times. This is true also regarding members killed at a worship service in Pittsburgh's *Tree of Life Synagogue.* Read David M. Shribman's article, *"Anti-Semitism in a City of Tolerance", The New York Times,* October 29, 2018.

Others have witnessed suffering death through lingering illness. It is painful to watch someone we love suffer while we attempt to offer comfort. Perhaps you too were empathetic when you heard or read about 15-year-old Benito Agrelo, who underwent his first liver transplant surgery at the age of 8, then a second liver transplant five years later and was still in constant pain and discomfort. He begged family and doctors to leave him alone. He was literally sick of it all and wanted in his own way to exercise his "right to die," with dignity. The desperate Benito said, "Enough is enough." Death seemed sweeter than all this suffering. How could anyone not be moved by this young boy's outcry?

Or take the story of the Minneapolis couple, Richard and Helen Brown, who were found dead in their garage, with letters sent to friends explaining that as an ailing elderly couple they saw their quality of life rapidly deteriorating from arthritis, asthma and Alzheimer's disease. They chose suicide together and left their sizable estate of $10 million to charity. Was suicide justified in this case? The Browns had the financial means for the best of healthcare, but they thought it unwise to use their resources uselessly.

This is an important issue facing today's global society. How far do we want to stretch medical technology to prolong existence? In 1994, the Netherlands passed legislation that fosters active euthanasia. The Northern Territories of Australia legalized voluntary euthanasia limited to terminally ill persons. In the state of Oregon, similar legislation (known as Measure 16) was narrowly approved by the voters some years ago. Was Dr. Jack Kevorkian, a medical doctor who served time in prison for his viewpoint in these matters, simply ahead of the law and society by assisting suffering persons to their death? In retrospect, would we be more accepting of Kevorkian's medical action, if we were crusading pioneers to ease the suffering of the terminally ill? This topic continues to be an issue for public and personal discussion and debate for us all.

In light of these heart-rending events, do people of faith have a sufficient framework by which to evaluate their own thoughts and feelings? Is there a need for a fresh paradigm, a believer's model for the 21st century to guide us? Are we willing to accept a framework of faith that will lift us beyond the pain we see and feel? How do we intend to address the realities surrounding dying and death itself? What are the wisest loving ways to face dying and death as realistic believers? Are we willing to extend our discussions with the following affirmations?

First: Begin by acknowledging that death is part of living. Life and death are intricately woven together; this is the tapestry of our human existence. To live is to die; this fact faces every human being. The time, place and condition of our inevitable death is unknown, but the fact that it will happen is real. To believe that someday we could outrun the grip of death due to our expanding knowledge is unrealistic. To think that our bodies can be frozen and thawed at a future date as a kind of "scientific Lazarus" is also unrealistic. It is important to note that death will teach us about the ways in which we can enhance the gift of life by the grace of our Creator-God.

Actually, from birth to death, we are in a process of dying as well as learning to live more fully. Many of us have simply not looked at our "passages" though life in this way. The late Henri Nouwen, noted author and theologian, observed, "Our lives can be seen as a process of becoming familiar with death, as a school in the art of dying", as we learn to live more fully until we catch-up with God's timing for us. Nouwen reminds us that "in every arrival there is a leave-taking; in each one's growing up there is a growing old; in every smile there is a tear; and in every success there is a loss. All living is dying, and all celebration is mortification, too" (from his *Letter of Consolation*). The late Cardinal Joseph Bernardin expressed it this way in his closing hours of life: "As a person of faith, I see death as a friend, as the transition from earthly life to life eternal."

Second: The believer's hold on reality not only sees death as an integral part of living, but that facing death energizes us to live more fully. There is a real sense in which death can be a gift. In my life, I have had significant encounters with death. Let me share two of them with you.

My mother had cancer and died at the age of 51. The last 12 months of her life were filled with purpose for her and for me. My mother was a widow, and I was aware of the responsibilities ahead of me. My younger sister was in college and I was in my senior year at Princeton Theological Seminary. My mother wanted me to complete my studies. I was focused and energized in that senior year to make the most of each moment in spite of concerns for my family. My mother was focused and energized to hold on to life until I was able to return. I completed my studies and returned home, skipping the graduation ceremonies. Of course, I was angry about her cancer and couldn't understand what God had in mind. However, my mother and I believed that God had a purpose for us. We also understood on that June day in 1958 that all circumstances are never fully in our control. My mother died peacefully some hours after my return from the Los Angeles Presbytery gathering (known today as the Pacific Presbytery of the Presbyterian Church, USA) which examined and accepted me for ordination. I was at her bedside, and it was a holy moment for us.

Third: Facing death energizes us to live more fully. During my first year as an assistant pastor, I had an automobile accident while making a parish call. There were no seat belts in those days. The car was totaled, and after a long recovery period, I was thankfully healed. Surviving the accident fully from all indications was a miracle. Doris and I postponed our wedding for some months as advised by doctors. This experience reinforced my conviction that in the providence of God, I was being given another opportunity to serve and to redouble my stewardship before God. I could literally feel the energy of God's grace surging through me.

Dr. Daniel Callahan, well-known medical ethicist long associated with the Hastings Center, indicates in his book, *The Troubled Dream of Life: Living with Mortality (Georgetown University Press),* that life consists of many "little deaths" – death itself is an event foreshadowed during life. This fact enables us to regularly ask, *"Given that I shall die, how should I live?"* In other words, how should we live in the awareness that we shall die? As we integrate death with life, we will be energized to live more fully, making each moment precious with thanksgiving to our Creator-God for the divine grace that sustains us daily.

The reality of death also points out that we are finite and must accept the limits in which we live. Medical technology will not conquer death for us. To think otherwise is to live under an illusion. Dr. Callahan reminds us, "Death should be seen as the necessary and inevitable end point of medical care." Medical technology serves us best when it promotes both a good life and a peaceful death.

However, today we are placing medical technology in a Catch-22 situation, asking scientists to solve the "problem" of death or to assist persons to commit suicide. The medical system can't deliver satisfying answers. Think of popular television programs *ER* and *Chicago Hope,* which in some cases have been restructured under new titles and personalities today. Have you encountered doctors who have lost a patient? They are usually totally dejected, having lost the battle for life to which they are dedicated. Medical science cannot erase the biological fact of mortality. Even though progress zooms ahead, mortality cannot be eliminated. Indeed, we need to accept death as an important part of our living experience. When we see this relation between life and death, we will be able to serve more faithfully a caring and loving stewardship under God during our lifetime.

Fourth: Facing death provides time to reflect on God's calendar and purposes. Aging can be a powerful process of prayer and listening for wise decision-making among those we trust, seeking to be in sync with God's calendar more clearly. Jesus comforting Martha before awakening Lazarus from the dead, reminded her of this with compassion, "I am the resurrection and the life. Those who believe in me, even though they die will live, and everyone who lives and believes in me will never die." (John 11: 25-27)

As believers facing reality, our task is to accept death when it occurs and to turn moments of "little deaths" into opportunities for greater service and dedication to our Creator-God, the Author and Finisher of our lives. To think that we can completely control the death process with the aid of medical technology is a delusion and even dehumanizes those caring for us. There are times in life when God rudely awakens us to our limitations; calling us to walk by faith, not by a technician's will that extends suffering without merit. We are primarily called to act and care for one another with compassion, seeking to act within our limited skills, as witnessed in the hospice movement. *We need to find the balance between the caring and curing of people.* Medical technology has directed our primary attention toward cures, and perhaps we have underplayed the importance of caring, when curing no longer is a viable option. Losing the balance between caring and curing is costly in our over-medicated society, overlooking the extensive suffering of poverty and displaced lives in our neighborhoods and in the distant corners of the world. Faithfulness through death brings awareness that we are all embedded with the spirit of the *imago Dei* that teaches us three realities with every breathe we take:

> *Lesson One: Living is part of dying*
> *Lesson Two: Dying is part of living*
> *Lesson Three: In life and in death,*

317

we belong to God.

(Inspired from the *Brief Statement of Faith*, PCUSA)
Scripture to consider:
Psalm 55-56; 103, 139-142, 143-145, 146-150
Micah 6:8 *"And what does God require of us--justice, kindness, love & humility."*
John 11:25-27 & John: chapters 17 and 21
Matthew 18:1-9 (Defining greatness) & 25:31-46 (Our Inheritance)
Galatians 3:28-29 (Uniting believers—a process with its struggles)

Books and articles for classroom and neighborhood discussions:
Robert K. Hudnut, *Meeting God in the Darkness,* Regal Books, Ventura, California

Atul Gawande, *Being Mortal: Medicine and What Matters in the End,* Metropolitan Books, New York. See *PBS Frontline Documentary* on *"Being Mortal".*

Daniel Callahan, *"The Desire for Eternal Life: Scientific Versus Religious Visions",* The Ingersoll Lecture 2002-03, *Harvard Divinity Bulletin,* Spring, 2003

Nellie Bowels, *"ETERNITY in a Tree—A start-up looks to forests to redesign the entire end-of-life experience",* *The New York Times,* June 13, 2019.

Ken Murray, *"Why Doctors Die Differently"*, *The Wall Street Journal*, February 25, 2012. Dr. Murray states that medical doctors have learned the limits of treatment and understand the need to plan for the end.

Pagan Kennedy, *"To Be a Genius, Think Like a 94-Year-OLD"*, *The New York Times*, April 9, 2017. "We assume", indicates Kennedy, "that creativity and innovation belong to the young. We're wrong" *The New York Times*, 4/9/ 2017.

William E. Phipps, *"Christian Perspectives on Suicide"*, *The Christian Century*, October 30, 1985. See also Jo Craven McGinty, *"Around the World, Suicides Rise in Spring"*, *The Wall Street Journal*, April 20-21, 2019.

Robert Powell, *"Before Passing Along Valuables, Pass Along Values"*, *The Wall Street Journal*, 12/ 10/2012. Useful article for discussion & planning one's will.

2019marked the twentieth anniversary of the Columbine school killings. See Tawnell D. Hobbs, *"Three Decades of Shootings: An Analysis" in The Wall Street Journal*, April 19, 2019. *The* vast *majority of voting Americans want change, and the next generation of youth agree.*

Chapter 24. Biblical Questions beyond Quizzes

Life's journey is filled with numerous questions and incomplete answers that occur daily. Learning that matters links competing tensions between questions and answers heard often during the Coronavirus Crisis and other pandemics, influencing public policy and public safety as Americans face a major election. Responses to enquiries are partial in nature as an effective vaccine is sought for the global population. The processes of discovery must be honest and responsible.

Every generation has its claim to "greatness" measured by scientific advances, war-time victories for freedom and educational accomplishments to understand ourselves better in the midst of diversity and distrust in human affairs. But we continue to live as a global community within the shadows of nuclear fear and peace talks backed by military force that doesn't quite seem ready with itself or peacemakers not in sync with each other. No doubt we spend more on protecting ourselves than building peace. Each side of the equation is costly while every nation creates its list of priorities. Peace-making seems almost impossible with every nation seeking pseudo-greatness. Actually, there can be no true greatness without honest and fair attempts to reduce the high cost of supporting our suspicions of each other, a hidden "military cost" that could be redirected to improve the declining lifestyle of citizens and families in matters of health and education. We are all called to be stewards for the common good created as we are in the *imago Dei, in the image of God to care for each other nationally and globally.* Why then do we harbor so much anxiety within us, feeling alone and isolated from nations and relationships around the world?

Do we need to be dictated by our nuclear age rather than follow a fuller and wiser vision sanctified by God's love for humankind and created life. Our Creator's ambition encompasses a family of nation that surpasses our tribal outlook with resources in abundance under careful stewardship faithfully administrated with a universal outreach and generous outreach that reflects an American Spirit of kindness and openness that envisions global greatness to share the abundance of talents we have to strengthen the world to care for each other for the sake of peace, justice and prosperity that embraces the world now and envisions the universe next on God's calendar for greatness.

Mister Rogers' television shows produced originally in Pittsburgh with its theme "Won't You Be My

Neighbor?" continues to be relevant. This theme is expanding in other formats such as CBS's "God Friended Me", transforming Mister Rogers' theme to *"Won't You Become My 'Universal Neighbor'?"* It is also interesting to note that Fred and Joanne Rogers resided in the Squirrel Hill neighborhood of Pittsburgh near the Tree of Life Synagogue where the tragic killings took place. Are we in the process again of distancing ourselves from neighbors locally and globally? Have we forgotten so quickly that what is local becomes global in our interconnected and interdependent world undergoing constant change? What future is there in de-globalizing ourselves as well as the global excellence of higher education that international students admire around the world? Isn't that going backwards for citizens with a vision to prepare themselves to possess *Heaven's Passport for a fuller life on earth* to envision God's destiny not only for ourselves, but for humankind as well working together as soul-mates as become a universal society as well as global society honoring our Creator-God. neighborhood discussions on biblical passports for common unity and enrichment.

Why are we willing to forsake the potential betterment of our lives in an emerging global society, by building more walls for isolation? A gated world provides false security by disconnecting our everyday lives from the safety required with open streets as we come and go freely without fear and anxiety. Being connected and supportive of one another is a wiser and more enduring approach to uphold the spirit of the *imago Dei* wherever we live. Stubborn biases can trigger the next apocalypse out of anger and distrust. A major blast can ignite disaster anywhere, blinded by hatred and consumed by fear. Fred and his wife Joanne, our friends for many years in Pittsburgh, have a meaningful grasp of building goodwill relationships within communities as they attended the Sixth Presbyterian Church in Squirrel Hill. The diversity of their neighborhood enriched their lives as they became acquainted with many cultures, beliefs

In my teenage years, I had a pastor who was concerned that I asked too many questions on human nature--why do we do what we do? On one occasion, he said, "Where is your faith? You ask too many questions." I recall sharing that remark with high school classmates. They invited me to attend Bible studies at their church. Their pastor's style of teaching was based on exchanges with the young people, a question and answer approach to learning. He encouraged my classmates to express their doubts and encouraged curiosity, engaging us all in a non-dogmatic way to strengthen our faith together. It was actually this Socratic method of learning that influenced me later to join the Presbyterian Church tradition. I wanted to have fellowship with enquiring believers where questions were welcomed. From my study of the Bible, I adopted a similar teaching style in the classroom, which works well with distance learning as well. I also thought of it as being close to the way Jesus taught with parables and rhetorical questions when questioned by the authorities of his day.

Centuries later, the famous German philosopher Immanuel Kant designed his own parallel set of questions for students, using a teaching style similar to Jesus as reported in Scripture. (Matthew 4:1-11). Kant raised three significant categories of questions often asked by humans young and old during their lifetime as follows: **(1) What may I know? (2) What ought I to do?** and **(3) What may I hope?** Kant believed that answers to these three questions would help to further our purposes and motivate us to be caring soul mates to one another in the course of our lifetime.

First, what may I know in life? How reliable is the information we learn in leading us to the meaning of life? In many introductory philosophy and theology courses this primary question is referred to as the epistemological issue. *Namely, how do we know what we know?* This question is certainly just as relevant today as it was for Kant. Think of the many possible pathways to knowing anything in life today. Our commitment to research beckons us to have an open mind in all fields of study. Also, we learn to value the knowledge gained from personal experience, field tests, and lab research. We also learn from the experiences of others who have lived before us. For instance, we watch someone bite into a steaming hot pizza, and quickly see how that person reacts in pain. Our senses of touch, hearing, sight, smell, and taste inform us daily of many realities. The experience of affection leads to understanding love. The experience of anger and hate alerts us to the darker sides of reality. Experience plays

325

a significant role in shaping our learning, listening, and observing process.

Knowing can also extend beyond experiences, study and discussions. We also learn by rational deduction or logic. Reasoning itself is an endless means of testing what we know and paves the way for later reinforcement or revision based upon further evidence and data. Albert Einstein's formulation of relativity was at first a rational mathematical discovery that later was verified by experience and data that strengthened his deductions.

There is also an intuitive way of knowing, a hunch or a feeling that leads us to study and detect other avenues based on intuitive insight. There are also other possible avenues to pursue a mystery like a detective or scientist focused intuitively on one or more areas uncovering information of significance. This way of knowing may be subjective and more difficult to ascertain. Those now searching for a vaccine for the current pandemic may in their research pursue a real hunch that works.

Another way of knowing today is through artificial intelligence (AI). Data is essential to organizations and business in such matters as design, distribution of products and building materials. Graduate students in business schools are exposed to its potential value, realizing that "our bodies can only be in one place at a time, but data can be in multiple locations at once." See what Atossa Araxia Abrahamian has written, *"We're All*

Data Subjects", *The New York Times*, May 29, 2018. We are also entering into a new *era of "Data Religion"* that provides not only information, but also advances human insights and values. Will knowledge seekers in the humanities including religious studies engage in "data religion" along with colleagues and fellow students in science, environmental studies, medical, law and economics?

In what ways can we anticipate benefiting from the knowledge and application of data? Will data studies also be helpful in designing our biblical passports? Such questions might seem far-fetched when we note the limited use of data in theological studies. However, we are all encouraged in this new era of abundant data to allow it to influence all walks of life. See David Leonhardt's review in *The New York Times* 6/10/18) on the future role of data, from a recent book entitled, *Reinventing Capitalism in The Age of Big Data,* by Viktor Meyer-Schonberger and Thomas Range (Basic Books). Information is constantly increasing in *AI*. See also the special section published by *The New York Times on Artificial Intelligence,* October 19, 2018 and Hannah Fry's recent book, *Hello World: Being Human in the Age of Algorithms,* Norton & Company.

Understanding one another's *Spiritual DNA,* can also be a passageway to communicate trust-building in our lives. Ours is an interdisciplinary age. There are many surprising levels of discipline to discover each other while slowly admitting openly and wisely our history of past errors, uncovering a new willingness to accept on another's "algorithmic citizenship". Artist James Bridle writes this brief description in *Citizen Ex.* a browser extension with websites to ascertain where the new data is "from" and "why". Our prejudgments at times have been incorrect. Every believer's way of knowing can extend beyond our current learning experience, reasoning and intuition. It may even involve an intuitive hunch with added prayer that leads to a unique disclosure that escaped researchers earlier.

Such insights enable us to accept our Bibles as a sacred text with its divine roadmaps interpreting *God's Will,* as we question past interpretations and conclusions. Scriptural study can be refreshing, leading to new questions while also reviving yesterday's wisdom. Its symbolic authority in courts still calls us to take an oath on the Bible, to tell the whole truth in the courtroom and when sworn into public office. In other words, the Bible challenges our finite remarks. John Calvin, a respected theologian in history was instrumental in shaping the spiritual and ethical foundations for the City of Geneva, Switzerland. Calvin considered his study of Scripture, as the *School of the Holy Spirit*, inspiring readers and listeners to be faithful to God throughout lifetime.

Calvin believed lives ought to be nourished in Holy Scripture and fashioned into governance by the light of the Holy Spirit. While we won't be perfect, we need to cultivate nevertheless a forgiving and loving attitude toward God and one another. God knows more than we do as we face actual realities in life. This is why God, not us, holds the final decision or judgment on our lives. This explains in part why Calvin indicated in his *Institutes of The Christian Religion* that, ***"True wisdom consists of two things: knowledge of God and knowledge of self."*** A complete understanding of both may be beyond us, as we review our checkered history of beliefs and denials practiced during the course of our lifetime. I suspect most of us have been fickle in our faith practices whatever our faith tradition might be-- Jewish, Christian, Hindu, Buddhist, Muslim, etc. within the dynamics of a changing world. Do leaders and scholars have complete histories of the changes taking place among their followers? If we did, we could strengthen the common ground that pulls us together and build trust across our religious divisions as we address life issues like Covid-19 that affects us all in some way. Whatever our faith tradition, sharing together builds the collective spirit of the *imago Dei* in us to act wisely.

How many of us today believe it possible that a major event of goodwill supported by diverse religious followers globally with past histories of distrust would enable us to honor each other's humanity advancing the spirit of the *imago Dei embedded in us.* This is what we need if we wish to live together in peace with justice and prosperity for all. It calls on all of humankind to risk working together for a healthier world, transcending our tribal ignorance that imprisons us within self-proclaimed borders and weakens us from following a larger vision of goodwill together.

A second significant question of life is, "What ought I to do?" Most of us wish to act ethically--to practice mutual standards of decency in the marketplace and in our social relationships. We are aware that there exist many gray areas with conflicting values that require constant examination, if we wish to act together in an inclusive manner.

In Micah 6:6-8, the prophet informs us of God's expectations with these questions that fulfills the divine will embedded in the imago Dei: my *"Shall I come before God with burnt offerings, with calves a year old? Will the Lord be pleased with thousands of rams, with ten-thousands of rivers of oil? Shall I give my firstborn for my transgressions, the fruit of my body for the sin of my soul?"* Then the prophet repeats with firm conviction the answer to his questions, **"God has showed you what is good; and what does the Lord require of you, but to do justice and to love kindness and to walk humbly with your God."** These are the sacred standards expected collectively of us all during our journey through life.

Theologian Robert McAfee Brown in his book *Spirituality and Liberation* (West- minster John Knox Press) puts these verses from Micah into a visual format for us: **"To act justly--to love tenderly--is to walk humbly with God."** These three actions are interrelated and interdependent; to act justly, to love tenderly, to walk humbly with God. We are all presented with this ethical triangle-- each side of the triangle needs the other two. We might start with justice, love or humility, but we can't progress far without the support of the other two sides that complete the ethical triangle. Most teaching based on biblical ethics consists in strengthening each link of our ethical triangle-- (1) justice, (2) love and (3) humility—all sides must be submissive to God's Will to transcend the pressure to do only what is expedient.

This brings us to the third question, namely, **"What may I hope?"** The biblical response is found in I Corinthians 15:12-19, where the Apostle Paul teaches believers that hope is not simply related to the resurrection story of Jesus, but far beyond to the mountain tops ahead. The Apostle Paul highlights in his epistles, that if there is no resurrection of the dead, then Jesus has not been raised, and if Jesus has not been raised, then our teaching amounts to nothing, and our faith is in vain. It is God's Will that desires a continuous relationship with us since we are reconciled and nurtured in forgiving love. This is God's plan to maintain a continuous fellowship with us in our journey of life.

Nikos Kazantzakis, author of *Zorba the Greek* and other noted books, did not center his total sense of hope in the resurrected Jesus. In fact, he found himself writing that the last temptation to be overcome in life is hope itself.

He felt that Christian hope deceives us from accepting the necessity of death. Visiting the island of Crete, Doris and I had the opportunity to see the gravesite of Kazantzakis, with the epitaph on his grave that states: "I hope for nothing. I fear nothing. I am free." This was his response to the major questions of life. For him, liberation meant freedom from hope and fear.

What epitaph might we write for ourselves? Would your epitaph express your essential beliefs? How honest would we be? Would your comments agree with Kazantzakis? *My epitaph would read: "I hope in Christ. I fear nothing. Therefore, I am free."* Christian liberation stems from our hope in Christ, not from the absence of hope. Contemporary theologian Jurgen Moltmann states it concisely, ***"to hope is* human and to hope in Christ is to be Christian."**

We have been discussing the three significant questions of life that confront us all: *(1) What may I know? (2) What ought I to do? and (3) What may I hope?* Our responses to these major questions of life will have its lasting value. No doubt some are still searching for answers to their own questions and still unwilling to reveal what's hidden in their hearts. The above questions nevertheless are worth discussing, as we design our biblical passports, and review the pathways your neighbors have already chosen. Many of us may still be seeking new adventures, as ambassadors of goodwill in an expanding world, or perhaps we choose to remain nearer to our homes and communities where we have invested so much of our talents and services. Our current stance in these matters may not be the end of our journey, as God continues to suggest doors we never expected. May we uncover joy beyond our dreams, as we approach opportunities with our biblical passport of choice in hand.

This closing chapter is dedicated to my sister Elizabeth Calian, known lovingly as Aunty Liz to our family. She had wonderful years as an elementary school teacher with her artistic talents. She died in August 2019 having declined in health over the last decade, upheld by her faith, friends and family.

Scripture to consider:
Genesis 1:24-31
Deuteronomy 8:7-18
Job 14:14, 17-29
Psalm 14:1-7; 37 & 38
Ecclesiastes 4:4-16 Does life end with vanity & running after the wind? *& 7:11-20 Why destroy yourself?*
Isaiah 11:1-10
Micah 6:6-8 (What do we bring to God?)
Matthew 20:17
Acts 9:1-7; 17:22-31
I Corinthians 15:12-19 & II Corinthians 3:17--4: 12
Colossians 3: 9-17 On becoming soul-mates thanks to God's grace
II Peter 3:1-18 How to stay awake when you should.

Articles and films on life's meaning for discussion:

Bryant M. Kirkland, *"The Fool Hath Said"— 'There Is No God'" A Sermon* preached by the former pastor of The Fifth Avenue Presbyterian Church, who I was fortunate enough to have as my mentor in ministry during my student days at Princeton Theological Seminary

Tony Campolo, *"Seeking to Stand Where Jesus Would Stand: The Price for Accepting Gay Couples into the Church"*, *Christian Ethics Today,* Fall, 2015. Professor Campolo is currently Co-Director of the Red-Letter Christians Movement.

Jacoba Urist, *"The Gospel of Minimalism: Real life realities can also get in the way of a minimalist religion. And despite some benefits, having less doesn't always lead to nirvana."* The New York Times, Thursday, May 4, 2017.

Professors Gary Marcus and Ernest Davis, *"A.I. Won't Fix Fake News"*, *New York Times, October 21, 2018*

David Brooks, "Fighting Suicide Is A Collective Task", *New York Times, 3/15/19*

Campbell Robertson, *"31 Doctors, 32 Million Pills: Prosecutors Detail Charges in Sweeping Opioids Case"*, *New York Times, 4/15/19*

Designing Your Biblical Passport for a Fuller Life

"Will You Be My Neighbor?" A film based on Fred Roger's TV programs. Actor Tom Hanks plays the role of Fred Rogers.

This movie *"First Reformed"*, is focused on an anguished pastor faced with a dwindling flock in a fearful world. Paul Schrader's film is modeled in part after a classic book, *The Dairy of a Country Priest.*

The film **R. B. G.** is based on a book by Irin Carmen & Shana Knizhnik, *"Notorious RBG: The Life and Times of Ruth Bader Ginsberg",* William Morrow Publishers.

Jeneen Interlandi, *"Why We're Losing The Battle With Covid-19, The New York Times Magazine, 7/19/20*

Nicholas Kristof, *"We Interrupt This Gloom to Offer ...Hope", The New York Times,* July 19, 2020

Afterword

This shorter sampler of my Biblical Passport was published in the *Pittsburgh Post-Gazette.* Your local paper may accept yours as well. Mine appeared in the PPG Sunday Edition entitled,

Promoting Peace

THE IDEA OF A BIBLICAL PASSPORT came to me as I was examining my latest U.S. passport at home. Before me was my bookshelf with different Bible translations I have found useful in my reading of Scripture. It was then that I envisioned having my own biblical passport, consisting of several pages of Scripture and thoughts that would accompany me on my travels. My biblical passport would be brief in content, enabling me to commit basic points to memory for easy use as I seek to establish meaningful, respectful connections with people I met on my journeys. The following is ***my seven-point model of my biblical passport*** for use in my travels at home and abroad whenever it was helpful to use in getting acquainted with others.

1. **Start your day right (Psalm 139:23-24).** My biblical passport begins with this prayer: *"Search me, O God, and know my heart; test me and know my thoughts. See if there is any wicked way in me and lead me in the way everlasting."* This is my morning prayer. My quiet time also includes scriptural readings, reflections and thanksgiving to God for another day of grace, whatever the weather might be. *New Revised Standard Version*

2. **Treat individuals as sacred (Galatians 5:6).** Getting acquainted with strangers is an essential first step in developing partnerships and discovering values that are shared, even if they're expressed differently and influenced by different backgrounds. I find it interesting to learn about other cultures. We are called to nurture and enjoy not only our families and friends but also to enrich our circle of fellowship to include strangers and even those who are our competitors and enemies. Otherwise, what real chances have we for lasting peace, prosperity or justice as a global community? Paul's Letter to the Galatians- often referred to as the *Magna Carta of Christian Liberty*-reminds us that in Christ, "Neither circumcision nor uncircumcised avails anything, but faith working through love" *King James Version*

3. **Be generous (Acts 4:32 – 5:11)** In the Acts of the Apostles, we learn that the early community of believers was strengthened and grew through its spirit of generosity. Property and other possessions were given to the community to sell and the general funds distributed according to each member's need. Commitment to one's "biblical passport" will promote generosity and a willingness to meet community responsibilities. *The Message: The Bible in Contemporary Language*

4. **Practice moderation (Galatians 5:22-23)** It can be said that we are as ethical as the last time we were tempted. None of us is immune. Obsession in its many forms seems to trump our best intentions. However, when we reflect on the importance of moderation, as Scripture encourages us to do, we find ourselves tasting the fruit of the Spirit – "love, joy, peace, patience, generosity, faithfulness, gentleness, and self-control. *New Revised Standard Version*

5. **Disclose mistakes (Mark 4:22-28)** Confession and restitution are necessary to restore ethical character in the global community. In Mark's Gospel, Jesus warned his disciples, "For there is nothing hidden but it must be disclosed; nothing kept secret except to be brought to light. If anyone has ears to hear, let him listen to this." *The Jerusalem Bible.*

6. **Speak briefly and act wisely (I Kings 3:27-28)**
Lies are endemic to our lives; even etiquette fosters deceit in our relationships. Speaking the truth is an effort to do the right thing by all persons involved. To act wisely in delicate matters affecting the lives of others requires that leaders stay well informed and act on facts, not rumor or anger. Having all the evidence may be impossible, but we are obligated to maximize our knowledge as a prerequisite for coming to a just judgment. In the days of King Solomon, two women fought over a baby, each claiming to be the child's mother. Who was telling the truth? Solomon listened silently. Then he asked for a sword and ordered the baby cut in two, so half could be given to each woman. The true mother, loving the child too much to see it killed, pleaded with the king to give the baby to the other woman. And then Solomon said, "Give the living baby to the first woman; do not kill it. She is its mother." And the people of Israel saw that their king had divine wisdom and the ability to administer justice. *The New English Bible*

7. **Don't quit on God, others or yourself. (Psalm 138)** When the waters of life are stormy, we have the scary feeling that perhaps God is absent. En route to Antarctica on an educational trip, my wife and I were sitting in the ship's library. I was preparing the next day's worship service as one

of the chaplains when we saw two 80-foot waves strike the ship. Library books fell, and tables were overturned. It was indeed a frightening experience. The ship was like a cork surrounded by high waves as the dedicated captain and crew made every effort to head back to port some distance away. Amid the anxiety and fear, many found themselves praying. The next day after calm set in, we experienced an overflowing worship service in the ship's theater to everyone's joy. The "Easter Crowd" was back at church. For a moment, we had the passing thought that God had quit on us.

We may have neighbors and family members who feel like that today with their economic fears, job concerns, poverty, and health issues including the loss of loved ones from the coronavirus pandemic. When I was nine or ten years old, finances were tight for my Armenian immigrant parents trying to make ends meet in America, where my sister and I were born. Hope seemed far away. Then one day, returning to our rented flat, I found a large unmarked package outside the door. I asked our neighbors, but no one expected any package. For some time, we kept thinking someone would claim it. Eventually, we opened it and saw that it was a large family Bible. We took it as a divine sign of hope and love that lifted our spirits. God had not quit on us. The underlying question in life, however, remains for all of us: How faithful will we be when tested to serve God, Others, or Ourselves first? What will our actual priorities be under pressure?

My model of a biblical passport closes with an abiding note of comfort in the midst of many unanswered questions; namely, to begin and end each day in a spirit of thanksgiving to God reminding ourselves that we live by divine grace surrounded by loving relationships – divine and human –revealed to us in surprising ways. It is these spiritual realities of faith that enable us to face our journeys in life *empowered not to quit on God, others, or ourselves* when tempted. This is why the psalmist in Scripture prays to God so powerfully: "When I walk into the thick of trouble, keep me alive in the angry turmoil. With one hand strike my foes; with your other hand, save me. Finish what you started in me, God. Your love is eternal--don't quit on me now." **Psalm 138:7-8, *The Message: The Bible in Contemporary Language*,** translated by Eugene Peterson.

The Next Page, April 6, 2014

Appendix I: Is There Illiteracy About the Bible? A Quiz

In memory of Rev. John Zingaro who organized the data from our conversations, while John was undergoing cancer treatments at the nationally known Hillman Cancer Center in Pittsburgh. John is a graduate of Pittsburgh Seminary and was serving a pastorate, when he found it necessary to leave and undergo care for his health needs. As a seminarian John was pursuing his second career; in his first career, John was a journalist. Answers to the quiz can be found in Appendix III.

1. What is the word that can be used to describe any writing in the Bible?
  Book Gospel
  Epistle Prophecy
2. Do all Bibles contain the same number of writings?
3. What languages were the Old and New Testaments originally written in?
4. What language did Jesus speak?
5. What does the word "Gospel" mean?

6. What does the word "Psalm" mean?

7. What is the difference between a disciple and an Apostle?

8. How many Apostles were there in total?

9. Do "Christ" and "Messiah" mean the same thing? What do they mean?

10. How many stories of Creation are there in Genesis?

11. Where in the Bible does it say that humans are made in the "image of God"?

12. Who was Moses' top assistant and successor?

13. How many psalms are there?

14. Chapter 13 from the First Letter to the Corinthians is often read at weddings ("Love is patient; love is kind..."). Who were the Corinthians?

15. Who was the first believer in Jesus to be martyred?

16. Solomon, the world's wisest man, was the son of...

    Moses   Abraham

    Jesus   David

17. Are the pyramids mentioned in the Bible?

18. The word "Deuteronomy" means "Second Law." Why is it called by this name?

19. Are John the Baptist and the Apostle John the same person?

20. Is the word "Trinity" mentioned in the Bible?

21. What is a parable?

22. There are prophets with similar names in the books of I and II Kings--Elijah as well as Elisha. Which one appears first?

23. Who are the characters in the Bible who never die, but are taken to God? Jesus, Elijah, Enoch, Moses

24. *The Battle Hymn of the Republic* has many biblical references. In which copy can references be found to "the grapes of wrath" and "the terrible swift sword"?

25. The opening aria of Handel's *Messiah* is "Comfort Ye." From which book of the Bible is this message found?

Appendix II: Ecumenical and Interfaith Dialogue in a Changing World

(1) Start an ecumenical dialogue group among interested neighbors from varied cultures, aim to be as inclusive as possible within your community. Gather in homes, backyards or nearby learning centers depending on health conditions for all. Frankly, there is no single way to get started. The important task is simply to begin with a few neighbors invited to discuss *the idea of designing one's own biblical passport for a fuller life where values and beliefs matter.* The beginning of this book can serve as an opener. Take turns leading, share responsibilities and engage in discussion together.

(2) Follow up on your initial exchanges and interests; expand your discussion topics with reading suggestions mentioned at the end of each chapter. Plan a group schedule to start designing drafts of your biblical passport.

(3) It may be difficult to design a meaningful biblical passport without having some time to know each other better. How long does it takes to nurture trust and build relations for useful exchange of ideas is difficult to say. Let's at least agree on a half-dozen or more sessions before measuring our progress, having learned by then more than we expected and enjoying it. It takes time to get acquainted.

(4) Church/State relationships and political issues will be raised with a diversity of viewpoints. Are we willing to be candid about our differences and keep the conversation going?

(5) After discussions, we may wish to give-up on designing a spiritual roadmap, which I consider to be one's biblical passport. Designing it may turn out to be a difficult task given our contrasting viewpoints that seem alien at times from our experiences and cultural differences in how we were raised. position. We might also find that each other's experiences offer unique and stimulating challenges to rethink the contents of our biblical passports, uncovering shared values among us.

(6) Is it too late for the religions of the world to unite for the sake of humankind? There are many different understandings of peace, heaven, justice, and faith that creates a confusing range of flags for us humans to fly on earth and find agreement among us.. Can it be true, that all of humankind is unique and yet created in the spirit of God's image, the *imago Dei?* I have had many opportunities beyond my formal education to be confronted with a wide exposure of human lives and cultures from my encounters, studies, and travels. Exposure to a range of subject material has encouraged me to be more interdisciplinary in my outlook, influencing me to rethink the educational process on all levels, and especially in relation to the future of graduate seminary education that would expose students and faculty to other fields of graduate and professional research and understanding that deepens all aspects of the *imago Dei* with the wonders of creation. Having seminary courses taught by a team of scholars that includes college, university, and research faculty can be enlightening for all involved. Such learning will become a unifying factor in educating tomorrow's global society that draws the faithful and talented from the world's religions closer together in advancing a larger vision of the *imago Dei* as our Creator-God hoped for benefiting humankind in goodwill together to further peace, justice and forgiving love to taste a fuller life together than we have known as our Creator-God intended from the beginning of time.

Every profession today needs to move beyond its comfort zones of learning, to grasp more fully the complexities of our lives within our expanding universe. With our moon shot achieved over 50 years ago (1969), now is our time to save planet earth by God's grace. Humankind is more wounded than we realize as we enter into this post pandemic era with fears, anxieties and displaced lives. *We feel more apocalyptic in attitude than hopeful.* But frankly, I don't believe God has forsaken us, instead we have been

349

given a awake up call to uncover the fact that we have forsaken ourselves with our distrust and greed.

(7) Wealth, health, and wisdom are factors of importance for the rich as well as the poor. Maintaining our physical & spiritual welfare includes funds and shelter as we learn to work together to fulfill God's Will in the spirit of the *imago Dei,* for the sake of humankind that calls for rich and poor to live in each other's skin. *Everyone is essential in becoming soul-mates to each other, fulfilling the* spirit of the *imago Dei. As we design our biblical passports, we may find that we have been privately discussing within our hearts the very theme of this book,* **Heaven's Passport for a fuller life on earth.** Would you be willing to admit it to yourself?

(8) Human history indicates that we have failed to secure lasting peace, meaningful justice, or universal prosperity. Some humans today are thinking of giving up on planet earth as they anticipate living in future space colonies with greater safety and security for themselves and future generations of their family. Is this the wisest way to plan for the future?

If God's Kingdom is our goal, then take note of the simple prayer that Jesus taught his followers: *"Thy Will be done Lord, on earth as it is in heaven."* (Matthew 6:9-13) *Jesus gave us the direct pathway for divine prayer, align yourselves with God's love that frees us from our stubbornness, offers us peace, justice, hope and abiding love that sustains us by God's grace.*

(9) An Interfaith Discussion: A sermon noted by Gandhi reminds us of God's horizon of hope for humankind. As a university student in England, Gandhi took notes from that sermon focused on social evils spoken at Westminster Abbey (3/20/1925) by an Anglican priest, Frederick Donaldson. Gandhi later recalled and published this in his weekly newspaper *Young India* (10/22/1925) highlighting the social ills found in human societies that Gandhi had encountered in South Africa as well as India which nurtured the roots of violence that he hoped to overcome during his lifetime.

THE ROOTS of VIOLENCE*
1. Wealth without work
2. Pleasure without conscience
3. Knowledge without character
4. Commerce without Morality
5. Science without humanity
6. Worship without sacrifice
7. Politics without principles

*From Micho Kaku's book, *Physics of the Future,* p.368

To further this interfaith and intercultural dialogue consider also these recent publications: Elaine Pagels, *Why Religion?,* HarperCollins; Barbara Brown Taylor, *Holy Envy*: *Finding God in the Faith of Others*, Harper One; and two *Christian Century* articles by Philip Jenkins, *"Compassion Gets Organized", 10/24/2018 & "Kenya rising",*4/8/2020. Jenkins writes that Africa will become the largest Christian continent with approximately a billion followers no later than 2040s. Also, Esau McCaulley, *"What the Bible Says About Rage"*, *The New York Times,* June 15, 2020 as we reflect on injustice at home.

(10) Importance of Honesty for Everyone: From *The New York Times* column of March 27, 2016, *"God is a Question, Not an Answer,"* Professor of Philosophy William Irwin at King's College, U.K. states that both an honest atheist and a true believer ought to be willing to admit that we all have periods of doubt, and can be wrong at times. For instance, there might be or not be a God after all, as envisioned within the realm of our finite knowledge on which we make an affirmative wager based on our convictions as did Pascal in his dialogue with skeptics. In today's context of diversity, we are all confronted with more significant questions than answers during the course of our lifetime. Nathaniel Hawthorne said of Herman Melville, "He can neither believe, nor be comfortable in his unbelief; and he is too honest and courageous not to try to do one or the other." Dwelling in a state of doubt, uncertainty, and openness about God's existence actually offers us an honest approach to many of life's ultimate issues. Such an attitude enables us to be honest in our search for authenticity in our conversations together. Perhaps we ought to follow Blaise Pascal's Wager, the French philosopher and scientist who had his own questions about God. Pascal argued that many persons in the course of their lifetime are willing to bet on either the existence of God or on the nonexistence of God. If one bets that there is a God and loses, nothing is lost. If there is a God, however, one's wager in life will be fulfilled beyond our calculations.

Those who claim to have certainty about their beliefs often worry quietly but prevent others from expressing doubts. When either side refuses to be completely honest, we undermine our ability to listen well, thereby losing beneficial insights in our mutual pursuit of truth. We can actually harm truthful friendships with sharp differences. Let's avoid putting limitations on God's grace to nurture us in our faith journeys in life. As finite humans, we might be wiser if we try to show more humility in our theological differences and be less heated in our political stubbornness as we discern the range of our priorities in life and why. Which priority interprets the other in our dialogue between theology and politics as we evaluate the quality and faithfulness of each other's stewardship to God? It may be more insightful to raise questions and discover perhaps the wide political gap that needs to be remedied on either side of issues to have meaningful peace. God's Will is to address our poverty of spirit which hurts rich and poor in their struggles together. We have often allocated resources and desires to satisfy our respective self-interests, failing to see the larger picture God has placed before us to succeed beyond each other's limited horizon. Recovering together the spirit of the *imago Dei* can be the beginning step in understanding God's true measurement of greatness with humility that enables us

353

to embrace God's vision for the totality of humankind that enables us to overcome short-sided perspectives that engage us in zero sum games that dehumanizes us in our destructive pathways.

Appendix III: Rethinking Seminary Education and Answers to the Bible Quiz

If your discussion group is interested in rethinking seminary education, you might consider inviting faculty and seminarians with their overseas guests in your area as well as clergy to participate in your conversations.

(1) First Amendment to the U.S. Constitution (1791)

"Congress shall make no law respecting an establishment of religion or prohibiting the free exercise thereof; or abridging the freedom of speech, or of the press; or the right of the people peaceably to assemble, and to petition the Government for a redress of grievances." What actually does the *separation of church & state* imply to citizens and noncitizens who reside in the United States? How free are we to speak and worship publicly? How free is the news media in keeping the public informed? Should fake news be restricted in a democracy? And what criteria have we to distinguish truth from falseness in our decision-making process? The First Amendment upholds our freedom and liberty as part of the U. S. Constitution which states

355

that *No State Sponsored Religious Faith* is required of its citizens and noncitizens. We believe simply in the separation of church (religion) and state (rule). Everyone is free to worship in the style and manner they wish. In political matters, the people and religious institutions have the right to "peaceably assemble, and to petition the Government for a redress of grievances." Is there a co-taught course on religious rights from its varied viewpoints (sacred and secular) being taught to seminarians, college and university students as well as to nearby laity for their understanding and stimulation as our public service to the surrounding communities that may wonder at times about the quietness observed at theological seminaries?

Thomas Jefferson sought to protect religions from government intrusion. The creation of his *Jefferson Bible,* in part, had this in mind. Are the religious concerns of evangelical, liberal or conservative believers of any faith tradition too constricted today? Each has the right to bring their concern to governmental authorities and the courts. For some, there is some feeling that there is religious restrictions on their political freedom, especially from the pulpit. Such feelings are often misplaced; religious institutions do have their freedom to discuss openly complex issues in contemporary society as an educational forum which most religious and secular institutions can provide, but such discussions are not to be confused with the sacredness and joy of divine worship which ought to have center-stage. The freedom of worship for all is at

356

the heart of our nation's priority to maintain religious freedom. *The United States has no state religion.* Politics can be discussed to keep its members and guests informed on national affairs as a forum for public discussion, led by informed and responsible citizens or guests on public affairs, but not in the context of a worship service where God's place has the highest priority for believers wishing to deepen their devotion and quiet their busy hearts in prayer. Political interests and loyalties can be discussed in a church or religious classroom or assembly hall with various viewpoints present for discussion. Have we been losing our spiritual compass today by debating our differences in the context of worship? Religious and political education ought to be in constant dialogue to nurture well informed citizens trusting in God and taking pride in their privilege to vote, can also speak freely on matters of public concern at the assembly hall later.

Politicizing the pulpit away from its scriptural base, in other words, and secularizing it for one's political interests can become its own form of idolatry, undermining our houses of worship dedicated to the glory of God. It is having this freedom of worship rooted in our U.S. Constitution that we wish to uphold.

Since faith and politics are closely related in American life, we tend to overlook over-lapping practices seen in national mottos and pledges. For example, have we discussed in recent times the use of God's name in allegiance to our nation? Are we willing to take steps to rekindle faith and national commitments as well pausing to understand the role of religion and its importance to citizens in a country that hasn't a state religion as in America? The emphasis in the United States has always been on our religious freedom with a high percentage of its citizens having some religious affiliation. Religion has played a significant role in American life even though there has been some decline in recent decades. The global population continues to see American citizens as religiously oriented although increasingly irregular in attendance before the pandemic started.

Do our mottos and our pledge to the flag that carries God's name still merit our support as well as our pledge on the Bible in court and on other significant occasions? Are these public rituals lacking realistic significance in our lives today? In short, do religious symbols add character to our lives as citizens? Do signs of our beliefs make a difference in how we live and behave in society? *Does it enhance our country and make a difference in how our lives are lived?*

These references to God, *"God Bless America"* and *"In God We Trust"* were officially voted upon by an act of Congress during the presidency of Dwight Eisenhower whose leadership was a major factor in the successful conclusion of World War II in Europe and Asia. The pledge and mottos in God's name remind us of our trust in the abiding values of or faith within a changing world. Will our emerging post-pandemic era of recovery be influenced positively as we repeat these national vows in tomorrow's world? Will our faith in God be necessary to maintain values as we travel across the country and around the world expanding into space and under the sea? Will our religious institutions and graduate seminaries be encouraged to invite believers as well as seekers to become students and further global awareness upholding humankind in the spirit of the *imago Dei?*

(2) Heaven

Are we aware of the many national flags that contain religious symbols that affirm some understanding of heaven as part of their national beliefs? What is your view of heaven? Some national flags display the moon in one of its phases; others have a crown or a cross. Have we read the brief discussions on heaven published in *Time Magazine* & the book *Spencer's Mountain?* Will the subject of "Heaven" be discussed as we design our biblical passports? Are we comfortable with expressions like "spiritual citizenship" and "citizenship in heaven"? Do we wish to have dual citizenship of country and faith as implied in our sacred texts? How do we respond to the many religious views of heaven visible among national flags globally? How do you react to the secular and scientific views in these matters expressed by the late Stephen Hawking and others with similar viewpoints. Hawking dismissed the idea of heaven in the *Guardian,* "I regard the brain as a computer which will stop working when its components fail. There is no heaven or afterlife for broken down computers. That is a fairy story for people afraid of the dark."

Hawking's view prompted Bishop N.T. Wright a recognized Bible scholar to respond in *The Washington Post* saying, "Of course, there are people who think of 'heaven' as a kind of pie-in-the-sky dream of an afterlife to make the thought of dying less awful." Wright wrote, "No doubt that's a problem as old as the human race. But in the Bible, heaven is God's space, while earth (or if you like 'the cosmos' or 'creation') is our space. And the Bible makes it clear that the two overlap and interlock." (Quoted in *"Rethinking Heaven", Time,* April 16, 2012)

"Lord, Miss Ida", laughed Clay. "The roof would fall in if I ever walked in that Baptist Church." "Don't joke about it, Clay," admonished Ida. "Don't you want to save your soul so you can go to Heaven and be with all the decent folks when you die?" "Miss Ida," said Clay, "the Baptists have got one idea of Heaven, and the Methodists have got another idea, and the Holy Rollers have got still another idea what's it's like, I've got my opinions, too." "I can just imagine what your idea of Heaven is," sniffed Ida. "A fishing pole and a river-bank." from *Spencer's Mountain* by Earl Hamner Jr.

(3) Theological Education in Tomorrow's World
On your next opportunity to visit a local library (or college, university or seminary library), look for a copy of the *Harvard Divinity Bulletin/ Winter 2017*

Bicentennial Issue which raises a number of probing questions regarding the future of theological education in North America and abroad. Among the questions being raised by clergy, laity and prospective graduate students is, *"What Is A Multi-Religious Divinity School"?* Would undergraduates and graduates' benefit from enrolling in such a school or to uncover similar type courses from their local college, university or theological seminary nearby that can stimulate us in preparing one's biblical passport, and can provide interfaith sacred texts and their histories to explore. This effort can lead to new information that you might be helpful in designing your biblical passport for global travel, as we prepare ourselves in understanding interfaith realities from the past and the present as we now begin to encounter new realities emerging from tomorrow's post-pandemic world and its impact upon the future dialogue among faiths and its followers.

Older methods of teaching world religions may no longer be sufficient. We will require an interdisciplinary approach to study the past as well as the present in our encounters with diverse professors and students from many faith and non-faith backgrounds to stimulate our thoughts and widen our outlook on the wonders of creation that awaits our discovery.

Tomorrow's comparative interfaith courses will be designed not just for seminarians, but for all institutions of learning offering research opportunities for students engaged in global matters--concerning faith, trade, religious disputes and innovative research that attracts diverse believers to study together in an interfaith world which is improving the lives of humankind with an emphasis on peace, justice, and goodwill following the footsteps of the *imago Dei as* foretold by our sacred texts. This emphasis will enhance interfaith offerings that will draw a wider audience to our theological institutions and also to courses in higher education that have an interdisciplinary emphasis. Hopefully there will be more team-offerings of classes in colleges, universities and seminaries held on their respective campuses combined with research trips in varied disciplines such as biblical archaeology, engagements with officials and programs in Washington D.C., the United Nations, the World Council of Churches in Geneva, officials in Rome and elsewhere around the world that relates to courses and disciplines at home.

A recent issue of *The Christian Century,* February 15, 2017 under the theme, "Remodeling Seminary" presents other thoughtful suggestions. Two shorter articles of mine were published in, *In Trust* a journal designed for administrators, faculty and trustees of theological schools. The two brief articles are, *"A radical proposal: Let's eliminate the M.Div."* (Part I Summer, 2014) and *"Let's learn to embrace new perspectives"* ("Part II Autumn, 2014). An earlier article of mine in *The Christian Century is "The Challenge of John 3;16 for Theological Education"*, February 5, 1986.

Francis X. Clooney, S.J., *"A Christian Pilgrim along the Buddhist Way"*, *Harvard Divinity Bulletin,* Spring/Summer, 2019. Professor Clooney teaches comparative theology at Harvard Divinity School.

Dennis Overbye, *"In a Remote Galaxy, a Black Hole That's Just Right"*, *The New York Times,* May 19, 2020.

Michiko Kakutani, ***"Pandemic Notebook"***, *The New York Ties Book Review,* May 17, 2020; Nick Palmgarten, ***"The Price Of A Pandemic: Pain and Profit on Wall Street"***, *The New Yorker, April 20, 2020; and also from The New Yorker, Alex Watt, "When This Is All Over" 4/13/20, and "Dispatches From A Pandemic", 4/1320.*

(4) Zingaro's Answers to the Bible Quiz
1. Book
2. No. For Protestants, the books of Holy Scripture consist of *66 basic writings with 39 books from the Hebrew cannon regarded as the Old Testament and 27 books for the New Testament.* Other biblical believers include *The Apocryphal/Deuterocanonical* Books that numbers 15 writings. All of these writings are included in the *Catholic Latin Vulgate* text accepted as their *Holy Bible.* The Eastern Orthodox Christians also have their varied versions of *Holy Scripture* with added variations of sacred texts based on Greek, Armenian, Ethiopic, and Syriac translations. There are also some Protestant churches (e.g. Anglicans) that include *The Apocryphal* writings within their *Bible.* To clarify our understanding

of these varied editions of the biblical material, I often refer readers to the *New Revised Standard Version (NRSV)* found in *The New Oxford Annotated Bible* edited by Bruce M. Metzger and Roland Murphy, published by the Oxford University Press.

3. Originally, the Old Testament was written primarily in Hebrew – with a few passages in Aramaic. A Greek version of the Old Testament was composed after the Hebrew original known as the *Septuagint.* The *New Testament* that followed was also written in common Greek.

4. Jesus spoke Aramaic a vernacular version of Hebrew.

5. Gospel means "good news," specifically "good news proclaimed in public" like the announcement of a town crier.

6. "Psalm" is a Greek word meaning "song."

7. All of Jesus' followers may be called "disciples." But only a small group was called by name to be Apostles. The word "apostle" is Greek, meaning a person who goes out and establishes a colony.

8. Fourteen. In addition to the original Twelve Apostles, there was Paul; Matthias was seen as a replacement for Judas – Acts 1:26.

9. Both "Christ" and "Messiah" mean "the anointed one."

10. There are two versions of Creation in the Bible from Genesis 1 and Genesis 2.

11. Human beings are created in the "image of God" is mentioned in Genesis 1:26

12. Joshua (became famous as the conqueror of Jericho)

13. There are 150 psalms. The Apocrypha and Eastern Orthodox add Psalm 151.

14. Corinthians were residents of the Greek port city of Corinth. Paul's letter is written to the emerging congregation recently formed at Corinth.

15. Stephen, one of the first deacons (Acts 7)

16. Solomon was the son of King David (as told in the book of I Kings).

17. The pyramids are not mentioned in the Bible. Some people believe that the storage silos during the time of Joseph (Genesis 40 and 41) were pyramids, but this belief is not established on any evidence.

18. Deuteronomy records the "second time" that the Law (the Ten Commandments and other laws) are explained by Moses to the Hebrew people as they are about to leave the desert and enter the Promised Land.

19. John the Baptist and the Apostle John are separate individuals. As told in the Gospels, John the Baptist introduced Jesus and his ministry; the baptism of Jesus signals the start of the carpenter's mission as the Christ. Later, Jesus chooses the fisherman named John as an Apostle.

20. "Trinity" does not appear in the Bible, though the three names representing Trinity do, as when Jesus selects followers to become disciples, he does so *"in the name of the Father, and of the Son and of the Holy Ghost"* (Matthew 28:19).

21. A parable literally means in Greek "a ball tossed to help," as if a story is told as a "by the way" illustration to help people understand a truth.

22. Elijah appears first, followed by his successor Elisha (I and II Kings).

23. Enoch and Elijah are taken straight to heaven (Genesis 5:24 and II Kings: 2:11). Jesus is taken to heaven (the Ascension--Acts 1:10) but only after dying and returning to his followers.

24. "The Grapes of Wrath" and "The terrible swift sword" are derived from the writings of the prophet Jeremiah (25:15-16) as a warning of punishment against the kingdom of Judah.

25. "Comfort ye" is from the writings of the prophet Isaiah (40:1) as God's way of assuring the Jewish people living in exile in Babylonia that their time of punishment had ended.

Epilogue

I came across "A Traveler's Prayer" written by Sir Francis Drake in 1577 on his journey to the west coast of South America as a tribute to the adventuring spirit of faith embedded in Eugene & Jan Peterson. They exemplified their own spiritual passports, emulating the spirit of Sir Drake—

Disturb us, Lord, when...
We are too pleased with ourselves, When our dreams have come true Because we dreamed too little, When we arrived safely Because we sailed too close to the shore.

Disturb us, Lord, when...
With the abundance of things we possess We have lost our thirst For the waters of life; Having fallen in love with life, We have ceased to dream of eternity And our efforts to build a new earth, We have allowed our vision Of the new Heaven to dim.

Disturb us, Lord, when to dare more boldly,

To venture on wilder seas Where storms will show Your mastery; Where losing sight of land, We shall find the stars. We ask you to push back The horizons of our hopes; And to push back the future In strength, courage, hope, and love. This we ask in the name of our Captain, Who is Jesus Christ. ***Francis Drake***

Note to our readers: ***Eugene and Jan Peterson*** joined us at Pittsburgh Theological Seminary in 1992, spending a year of their creative journey as our distinguish campus guests engaged in the early stages of their writing project, ***The Message: The Bible In Contemporary Language,*** published by NavPress.

Sam   and   Doris   Calian

About the Author
calian@pts.edu

Carnegie Samuel Calian was awarded emeritus status in 2006 following twenty-five years of service as president and professor of theology at Pittsburgh Theological Seminary, a graduate school of professional education associated with the Presbyterian Church U.S.A. He has earned degrees from Occidental College (BA in philosophy), Princeton Theological Seminary (BD in Divinity) and a doctorate in theology (D. Theol.) *magna cum laude* from the University of Basel, Switzerland. In addition, he received a certificate from the Advanced Management Program (AMP) at Harvard Business School and later invited as summer visiting scholar at Stanford University Graduate School of Business. He has also received five honorary doctorates from colleges and universities in the United States and Europe.

He has been associated with Juniata College, the University of Dubuque Theological Seminary, Oxford University's Harris Manchester College, Carnegie Mellon University and as a visiting professor at the Katz Graduate School of Business at the University of

Pittsburgh. In 2005, he was honored as the distinguished alumnus of the year at both Occidental College and Princeton Theological Seminary.

HEAVEN'S PASSPORT: For a Fuller Life on Earth is his twelfth book. He has also published 200 articles in journals and newspapers. He is married to Doris Zobian Calian, a former research chemist and graduate of the University of Pennsylvania. Together they are blessed with ten grand-children and their loving parents.

Acknowledgements

This has not been an easy book to write over the past few years, primarily due to the rapid change in technology which has made me feel at times that I was born in the wrong century, as I witness the advances that my children and grandchildren have experienced and mastered. I am grateful for their assistance and also the encouragement of editors and publishers from previous publications, the IT Department at Pittsburgh Theological Seminary and Ben Driver who was teaching Latin then at Shadyside, now in doctoral studies at Brown University. I am also glad for the editorial assistance of Jean Peters and Will Linder in Evanston, IL. There are so many others I would like to thank, including the excellent resources from librarians in Pittsburgh and Evanston. My appreciation also to Larry J. Martin for his patience and expertise in publishing this volume.

For the final completion of this book, I owe special thanks to the Calian and Trautvetter families --Lois and Dennis and our grandchildren (especially Paula and Caleb) who invited us into their home at the onset of the Covid19 pandemic. We certainly didn't anticipate that our "visit" would last for three months. Among their many sacrifices and kindnesses to us was their considerable technical knowledge. Paula's hours of labor enabled me to complete this volume. Anyone who knows me, will understand that this task could not have been finished without my loving wife Doris.

Carnegie S. Calian
July, 2020

Notes:

Made in the USA
Monee, IL
19 September 2020

42452278R00207